100

THINGS TO DO IN
ALASKA
BEFORE YOU
DIE

Denali National Park and Preserve
Photo courtesy of NPS, Jacob W. Frank

100

THINGS TO DO IN
ALASKA
BEFORE YOU
DIE

* *

FRAN GOLDEN AND MIDGI MOORE

REEDY PRESS

Library of Congress Control Number: 2020937338

ISBN: 9781681062921

Design by Jill Halpin.

Photos by author unless otherwise noted.

Cover photo by Debi Lander.

Printed in the United States of America
21 22 23 24 25 5 4 3 2 1

DEDICATION

This book is dedicated to the people of Alaska, who despite the COVID-19 pandemic and other challenges, continue to work hard and maintain a can-do spirit.

To Midgi's Father, Bud Gunter.
You are missed.

Tongass National Forest
Photo courtesy of USFS, Sheila Spores

CONTENTS

• •

History and Culture

• •

• •

• •

Photo Ops

• •

ACKNOWLEDGMENTS

Thank you to the sites, attractions, parks, and everyone else who helped us gather information along the way. A special thanks to Thompson & Company, Travel Alaska, and the Alaska Travel Industry Association, of which coauthor Midgi is a proud member. We'd also like to thank all the local tourist offices and attractions that helped us with information and fact-checking. Thank you to David Molyneaux, travel writer and Fran's husband, for his editing and insight.

PREFACE

Yes, we admit, it was really hard to pick only 100 great things about Alaska. To us, the whole state—well, at least the places you can actually get to—is a wonderland that warrants exploring. Of course, in a whole lifetime, you'll never see everything.

Our challenge was looking at the entire state, thinking hard about our favorite things to see and do, and making some tough decisions about what to include and what to leave on the table. In making our top 100 choices, we didn't just go with popularity nor, necessarily, ease of access—we included both close by and remote experiences, some of which are on our own future wish lists. Wintertime activities are part of our list, including places where it may be $-50°$ F or colder.

Among its undeniably impressive features, Alaska has more than half of the national parklands in the United States with 17 national parks, preserves, and monuments, and 16 wildlife refuges. These present a wealth of experiences, and they could fill a book by themselves.

Nature is not our only focus. We chose must-see places of historic interest, including those put on the map by the gold rush that drew stampeders here in the late 1800s and onward. (To this day, people still come to Alaska to seek their fortunes in gold!) We chose some sights for their super-fun kitsch value, restaurants that focus on sustainable Alaska products, must-do outdoor recreational

• •

experiences, and museums and villages where you can view priceless artifacts and gain an insight into Alaska Native cultures.

Our choices are designed to present a broad sample of Alaska experiences. Of course, some readers might not agree with everything. We're prepared for that—and who knows, if you write us and give us your ideas, they may appear in a future printing.

Please be aware we also had to work within our publisher's set format. So, for instance, if we don't mention every tour provider out there, it's not because there aren't other great companies. The information in the book was accurate at the time of publication, but businesses do close, and we urge you to check before you go.

Fran was raised in New England and now lives in Cleveland, but she's been coming regularly to Alaska for 30 years. She has written many Alaska-based articles and travel books to prove it. While most of her experiences have taken place in summertime and involve cruise ship travel (her specialty), a new obsession is winter in Alaska, when the tourists are few, there's a slower pace, the cold is good for the heart and soul, the Northern Lights paint the sky, and there is time to get to know more about real Alaska life.

Fran has attended Anchorage's Fur Rondy festival (a great celebration of all things Alaska); traveled the Dalton Highway in winter (stayed at Coldfoot); stopped by many towns, cities, and villages in Southeast Alaska; ridden the ski lifts at Alyeska; and experienced many Alaska restaurants and bars—and Alaska beers and distilled beverages. She's driven the Seward Highway and gone through the tunnel to Whittier, taken floatplanes to remote fly-fishing spots, bumped icebergs thanks to truly crazy (in a good way) small-boat operators, ridden rapids, visited the bears at Anan, gone dogsledding, hung out with master Alaska Native carvers, kayaked Glacier Bay (and several other places), and snorkeled (four times!).

Midgi Moore moved to Alaska from Utah to follow her captain and live the Alaska dream. She is married to Captain Grantley Moore, who runs Moore Charters and is our book's advisor on fishing experiences. Juneau is her adopted hometown, and she can't imagine living anywhere else. She opened her own company, Juneau Food Tours, in 2015, pursuing her passion for sharing insight into Alaska eating and the work of local chefs and food producers.

Among Midgi's other passions are culinary travel and building the industry she loves so dearly. She has been to every US state, but Alaska is her home. Her favorite places include Juneau, North Pole (because she loves Santa), and Fairbanks, which was her first Alaska home. She is particularly fond of salmon bakes and will stop at any she comes across.

With Fran's exploration over 30 years and Midgi's insight into her adopted home state, we hope we've captured the joy, lifestyle, and unmatched beauty of Alaska. Thank you for purchasing this book and coming along for the ride.

• •

Beer flight
Photo courtesy of Juneau Food Tours

FOOD AND DRINK

DINE WITH A TOP CHEF
AT 229 PARKS

Nominated multiple times for a James Beard Best Chef—Pacific Northwest award, and a contestant on Bravo TV's *Top Chef* season 15 (the first contestant ever from Alaska), Laura Cole has become the face of Alaska cuisine. Her focus is on the bounty of Alaska ingredients. For her restaurant, 229 Parks, just outside of Denali National Park, she works with small-scale farmers, beekeepers, ranchers, fishermen and fisherwomen, foragers, and other small-product food producers across Alaska. The restaurant also has its own 50-acre farm. Hard work and Cole's creativity show in signature dishes such as Alaska bouillabaisse and reindeer ragout with mint and house goat ricotta—plus, desserts such as beet and carrot macaroon ice cream sandwiches. Another must-try is the house-made sodas. This is a chef who is defining what Alaska cuisine is all about.

Milepost 229.7 Parks Hwy.
Denali National Park & Preserve, AK, 99755
229parks.com
(907) 683-2567

COMPETE IN AN ALASKA FOOD CHALLENGE
AT HUMPY'S GREAT ALASKAN ALEHOUSE

Humpy's Great Alaskan Alehouse in downtown Anchorage has an Alaska-sized food challenge that isn't for the faint of heart. As featured on the TV show *Man vs. Food*, the Kodiak Arrest Food Challenge consists of seven crab nuggets, 14 inches of reindeer sausage, four pounds of Alaskan king crab, side dishes, wild berry crisp, and ice cream. It costs $250, unless you can eat it all—in which case, it's on the house. You have 60 minutes to chow down the feast, and you can't leave the table while you're trying. Eat everything, and you get your name immortalized on the wall of fame and an "I Got Crabs at Humpy's" T-shirt. Spectators are encouraged to cheer on their champion and toast to their victory with any of the more than 50 taps of beer featuring everything from India pale ales (IPAs) to sours, barrel-aged stouts, and Belgians.

610 W. 6th Ave., Anchorage, AK 99517
(907) 276-BEER (2337)
humpysalaska.com

STOP BY
KITO'S KAVE

When you're looking for a dive bar, you want a place where you can drink local beer (or harder stuff) and converse with colorful locals. You don't want trendy—you want authentic. Kito's Kave, in the fishing community of Petersburg, is on historic Sing Lee Alley, up from Middle Harbor. You're likely to hear plenty of fish tales from the regulars. Don't take the stories or the rugged-looking fishermen at face value—fishing is prosperous in Petersburg, and some have made millions with their boats. Kito's is a big place. You can belly up to the bar to watch sports on TV, hit the pool tables, or head for the dance floor (there's sometimes live music and a DJ on weekend nights). Historic photos cover one wall. John Wayne visited Petersburg on his boat in 1967, two years after Kito's opened (it's not known if he visited the bar).

200 Chief John Lott Dr., Petersburg, AK 99833
(907) 772-3207
facebook.com/kitos.kave

ALSO CHECK OUT THESE DIVE BARS

Salty Dawg Saloon
4380 Homer Spit Rd., Homer, AK 99603
(907) 235-6718
saltydawgsaloon.com

Pioneer Bar
212 Katlian St., Sitka, AK 99835
(907) 747-3456
facebook.com/pages/category/Pub/Pioneer-Bar-
Sitka-Alaska-332938032854

Darwin's Theory
426 G St., Anchorage, AK 99501
(907) 277-5322
alaska.net/~thndrths

B&B Bar
326 Shelikof St., Kodiak, AK 99615
(907) 486-3575
facebook.com/BB-Bar-205971906087583

Van's Dive Bar
1027 E. 5th Ave., Anchorage, AK 99501
(907) 929-5464
facebook.com/vansdivebar

BREAKFAST
AT SNOW CITY CAFE

Alaskans like big breakfasts, and a lot of folks in Anchorage like theirs at the colorful Snow City Cafe, a local fixture since 1998. If you don't reserve ahead, you may have to wait in line for a table, but it's worth it. Or grab a stool at the counter and munch on a giant sticky bun while you wait. Coffee is served in assorted mugs donated by fans—when they run low, the owners put out word they need more, so your mug may feature someone's favorite sports team or alma mater (or it may say "I Love Mom"). Breakfast selections include eggs benedict with crab cakes or salmon cakes topped with house-made hollandaise, and eggs with reindeer sausage. A crab-filled omelet is another favorite, as are big plates of pancakes. Local art decorates the walls. Wine, beer, cider, and bubbly are available with brunch.

1034 W. 4th Ave., Anchorage, AK 99501
(907) 272-2489, snowcitycafe.com

Here are some other local favorite breakfast/brunch spots:

The Cookie Jar
1006 Cadillac Ct., Fairbanks, AK 99701
(907) 479-8319, cookiejarfairbanks.com

The Rookery Café
111 Seward St., Juneau, AK 99801
(907) 463-3013, therookerycafe.com

The Sandpiper Cafe
429 W Willoughby Ave., Juneau, AK 99801
(907) 586-3150, sandpiper.cafe

Cape Fox Lodge
800 Venetia Way, Ketchikan, AK 99901
(866) 225-8001, capefoxlodge.com

Glacial Smoothies and Espresso
336 3rd Ave., Skagway, AK 99840
(907) 983-3223, glacialcoffeehouse.com

Juneau Food Tours

EAT CRAB
AT TRACY'S KING CRAB SHACK

Tracy LaBarge, owner of Tracy's King Crab Shack, moved to Alaska in the 1990s. Her favorite thing to do was to go crabbing with her friends. She joked that one day she would open up a hot dog stand but sell crab legs "one leg at a time." Tracy's King Crab Shack debuted in 2006, tucked in an alleyway behind the Juneau Public Library. Serving huge and succulent Alaskan king crab legs, the business took off. A couple of tables became a dozen, and then a whole patio with a tent cover. Now Tracy's is an iconic Juneau restaurant, located on the waterfront and featuring the "best legs in town." Tracy also serves her award-winning king crab bisque, crab cakes, and the occasional fresh Dungeness crab. The shack has been featured in numerous culinary magazines and was a location for the "Quick Fire" challenge on season 10 of Bravo TV's *Top Chef*.

432 S. Franklin St., Juneau, AK 99801
(907) 790-2722
kingcrabshack.com

SAMPLE
MADE-IN-ALASKA FOOD PRODUCTS

Alaska offers a bounty of food products. Particularly popular are wild smoked salmon available in cans, jars, or vacuum-packed. A new favorite on the seafood scene is smoked octopus, by Kraken. Kelp is a staple on many an Alaskan's table, and Barnacle Foods creates kelp salsas, hot sauce, and seasonings. For something sweeter, pick up syrups, honeys, jams, or jellies made from wild Alaska blueberries, fireweed, and salmonberries. Keep life zesty with flavored seasoned salts such as Alderwood smoked, spruce tip, or blueberry. The blueberry is perfect for a berry margarita. After a long day, sit back with teas made from indigenous plants such as Devil's Club, which is known for its medicinal properties. Find the flavors of Alaska in gift shops in-state and online.

TIP

You can also taste Alaska products in coauthor Midgi's Juneau Food Tours' Taste Alaska! subscription boxes (see page 19).

CHECK OUT THESE PRODUCT PRODUCERS

Barnacle Foods
PO Box 21092, Juneau, AK 99802
barnaclefoods.com
(907) 957-4476

Alaskan Kraken
Salt & Soil Marketplace
1107 W. 8th St, Suite 4, Juneau, AK 99801
saltandsoilmarketplace.com
(907) 302-3841

Alaska Seafood Company
5731 Concrete Way, Juneau, AK 99801
alaskaseafoodcompany.com
(907) 780-5111

Alaska Wild Harvest—Birch Syrup & Honey
Mile 1.1, Talkeetna Spur Rd., Talkeetna, AK
alaskabirchsyrup.com
(800) 380-7457

Alaska Simple Pleasures—Jams & Jellies
Sitka, AK
alaskasimplepleasures.com
(907) 738-0044

SIP
49 BEERS

While breweries aren't new to the food and beverage scene, what makes Alaska breweries so special is that each one has its own take on using locally sourced ingredients such as berries and seasonal spruce tips. For instance, 34 years ago, Marcy and Geoff Larsen took a recipe from an old miner's cookbook, experimented a bit, and created their first beer—the Alaskan Amber at their Alaskan Brewing Company in Juneau. Seasonal beers include raspberry wheat and winter ale, as well as a summer blonde. Look for the limited-release pilot series that includes the Smoked Porter, which gets better with age.

Along with great beers, breweries are now creating hard seltzers and nonalcoholic options. Tap rooms are becoming family hangouts. The fresh glacier water in each barrel of beer brewed across the 49th state ensures smooth and fresh flavors.

Alaskan Brewing Company
5364 Commercial Blvd., Juneau, AK 99801
(907) 780-5866
alaskanbeer.com

VISIT
A DISTILLERY

Craft distilleries have made their mark in Alaska and offer beverages with unique Alaska flavors that include assorted berries, devil's club, and rhubarb—to name a few of the indigenous ingredients found in the small batches of gin, vodka, and whiskeys. At tasting rooms, which are popular hangout spots for locals and visitors alike, you can sample cocktails made with the spirits. Plan to take home a bottle or two.

The most recognized of the distilleries, Port Chilkoot Distillery in Haines, has won many awards, including American Distilling Institute's Best in Category for its London Dry-style 50 Fathoms Gin made with locally harvested spruce tips. Also prize-winning are its Wrack Line Rye, Green Siren Absinthe (made with such local herbs as wormwood and anise hysoop), and Boatwright Bourbon. They also produce Icy Strait Vodka.

Port Chilkoot Distillery
34 Blacksmith St., Haines, AK 99827
(907) 917-2102
portchilkootdistillery.com

HERE ARE ADDITIONAL PLACES TO WET YOUR WHISTLE AND PURCHASE LOCAL PRODUCTS

Amalga Distillery
134 N. Franklin St., Juneau, AK 99801
(907) 209-2015
amalgadistillery.bigcartel.com

Hoarfrost Distilling
3501 Lathrop St., Unit F, Fairbanks, AK 99701
(907) 479-6128
hoarfrost.vodka

High Mark Distillery
37200 Thomas St., Sterling, AK 99672
(907) 260-3399
highmarkdistillery.com

Skagway Distillery
941 Alaska St., Skagway, AK 99840
(907) 983-2030
skagwayspirits.com

Anchorage Distillery
6310 A St., Anchorage, AK 99518
(907) 561-2100
anchoragedistillery.com

SWING INTO
RED DOG SALOON

Juneau's Red Dog Saloon is noted in most guide books as a "must-go-to" place year round. As you swing through the doors, you are greeted with a rowdy "Hello!" Sawdust crunches under your feet, and the music from the old-time piano blasts throughout the room. Check out the memorabilia on the walls, and take a close look behind the bar for Wyatt Earp's gun. Order one of the many Alaska brews available on tap. If you're feeling adventurous, order a Duck Fart, which is a shot made with Baileys, Kahlúa, and Crown whiskey. "Quack, quack, throw it back" is the common toast to this smooth shot. If you're hungry, ask for a reindeer sausage pizza or halibut and chips.

278 S. Franklin St., Juneau, AK 99801
(907) 463-3658
reddogsaloon.com

ALSO CHECK OUT THESE
POPULAR DRINKING ESTABLISHMENTS

Imperial Saloon

Ask to see the history page. Robert Stroud, a.k.a. the Birdman of Alcatraz, once worked here.

241 Front St., Juneau, AK 99801

(907) 586-1960

facebook.com/pages/category/Bar/Imperial-Saloon-161181137262573

Red Onion Saloon

This former bordello is famous for ghost tours and fancy ladies.

201 Broadway, Skagway, AK 99840

(907) 983-2222

redonion1898.com

DRINK
A GLACIAL COCKTAIL
AT THE NARROWS

In the heart of Juneau is a very narrow bar called The Narrows. This former dive bar is only 1,000 square feet and with just 40 seats. Jared Cure, a local fellow who grew up in Juneau, purchased the bar after a decade of working in the Bay Area. The local story is that the previous owner just got tired of running the establishment, walked out, locked the door, and never looked back. Jared and his father spent nearly eight months renovating, and now it's the hot spot for late night cocktails. The Narrows began a trend of cocktails that include glacial ice. Jared works with a professional ice wrangler to bring in icebergs for special cocktails. Visitors can savor an elegant cocktail chilled with pure glacier ice said to be thousands of years old.

148 S. Franklin St., Juneau, AK 99801
(415) 205-3704
facebook.com/thenarrowsbaralaska

SNACK ON A FOOD TOUR
WITH JUNEAU FOOD TOURS

In Juneau, the old joke used to be that if you wanted a good restaurant meal, you needed to go to Seattle. That's no longer true, as the small capital city has more than 100 unique and eclectic places to eat and is making its mark as a culinary travel destination. Juneau Food Tours (owned by Midgi Moore, coauthor of this book) features the best in Alaska fare, particularly seafood. The tours are hosted by local residents who share the best places to dine, as well as fun history and facts about the city. Meet the local chefs, restaurant owners, and artisans who have built Juneau into a dining destination.

The state is filled with great seafood options, and many towns offer unique food-related tours. Whether you take a full food tour or something with small tastings, you can sink your teeth into Alaska.

2 Marine Way, #203, Juneau, AK 99801
(907) 723-8478
juneaufoodtours.com

TRY FORAGING
WITH A CHEF

Foraging in Alaska is an adventure. Both the forest and sea have a bounty of deliciousness from mushrooms, spruce tips, and countless berries to beach asparagus, kelp, and sea lettuce. Foraging is best with a local guide. On land, you are not alone, as you share the bounty with porcupines, marmots, eagles, ravens, and bears. Locals will know the best and safest places to hunt, and you might pick up a tip or two on making dinner. Chef Lionel Uddipa of Red Spruce in Juneau is well known for foraging for seasonal forest items on his menus. His young daughter and foraging partner is learning the technique of identifying what is safe to eat and when to pick it. She is often in the forest with her dad seeking the ripest berries or near the sea looking for beach asparagus.

Red Spruce
11798 Glacier Hwy., Juneau, AK 99801
(907) 500-5638
facebook.com/globalstreetfoodeatery

TIP
To schedule a private foraging experience with Chef Lionel or another Juneau chef, contact Juneau Food Tours (see page 19)

NOSH
ON REINDEER SAUSAGE

Reindeer sausage is an Alaska staple in restaurants and in most homes. Sausage is the most common reindeer product. Alaskans eat sausages served like the common hot dog, in a bun with a lot of mustard. Reindeer sausage carts are parked in popular areas throughout the state. When in Fairbanks, look for a local mustard called Moosetard, which is a good pairing with the zesty reindeer sausage. The sausage is also used in omelets, as a stand-alone breakfast meat, and on charcuterie plates. At the Red Dog Saloon in Juneau, it's the sausage on a pizza. Gift shops throughout the state sell reindeer sausage in shelf-stable packaging, allowing it to be safely stored at room temperature so you can take home a tasty souvenir. Visitors often ask about caribou. Reindeer and caribou are similar animals, but reindeer are domesticated, and caribou are wild, which is why you will find reindeer on the menu.

GO ON A BEER TOUR
WITH BIG SWIG TOURS

Explore the Last Frontier one brewery at a time with Big Swig Tours, Alaska's original beer tour company. Based out of Anchorage, Big Swig Tours has several options to quench your thirst. At the top of the list is Hops on the Rail.

Board the Alaska Railroad in Anchorage and enjoy the ride to Talkeetna and visits to up to four breweries. On a clear day, look for Denali, the highest mountain peak in North America. On the Alaska Crafted Tour and Train Adventure, you'll enjoy a leisurely train ride to Girdwood. Once there, take the aerial tram to the top of Alyeska for lunch. On your return trip, your Hoperator will escort you to several breweries for beer and cider tastings. Want to pedal and swig around Anchorage? Book an off-the-beaten-path bicycle tour for an afternoon of suds and a little exercise.

3113 Linden Dr., Anchorage, AK 99502
(907) 268-0872
bigswigtours.com

EAT IN AN AIRPORT
AT THE HANGAR ON THE WHARF

The Juneau waterfront is picturesque and easy to walk thanks to the city's boardwalk. At the end of the boardwalk is a blue building known as Merchant's Wharf (or "The Wharf" to locals). Stop in The Hangar on the Wharf Restaurant, grab a window seat, and order a burger and beer as you watch float planes take off and land from their charters to Taku Glacier Lodge. The restaurant is housed in an old floatplane hangar where, in the 1940s, the planes would land for fueling, washing, and repairs. The restaurant sticks to the aerial theme with historic photos mounted on the walls and model planes hanging from the ceiling. The menu features something for everyone, including fresh Alaska seafood as well as burgers, salads, and treats for the kids. It's the only downtown waterfront restaurant open year-round.

2 Marine Way, #106, Juneau, AK 99801
(907) 586-5018
hangaronthewharf.com

DINE
AT THE GOLD CREEK SALMON BAKE

Salmon bakes are among Alaska's most popular tourist attractions. The salmon isn't baked; it's grilled, often over an alder wood fire, and served with assorted side dishes and a campfire dessert of roasted marshmallows. The Gold Creek Salmon Bake, at the edge of a rainforest in Juneau, has been a favorite summer treat for thousands of visitors and locals for more than 30 years. The outdoor setting along a babbling creek lends a serene quality to dining. Take a short walk on the path to a waterfall or try your hand at gold panning. Be on the lookout for salmon in the creek and perhaps the bears, who enjoy the fishy buffet with the scoop of a paw into the creek. Talk with fellow travelers and diners, as it's not unusual to find yourself swapping travel stories and learning from locals.

1061 Salmon Creek Ln., Juneau, AK 99801
(800) 323-5757
alaskatraveladventures.com

ALSO CHECK OUT THESE SALMON BAKES

Taku Glacier Lodge
2 Marine Way, #175
Juneau, AK 99801
(907) 586-6275
wingsairways.com

Alaska Salmon Bake
2300 Airport Way,
Pioneer Park Mining Valley
Fairbanks, AK 99701
(907) 452-7274
akvisit.com

Sitka National Historical Park

HISTORY AND CULTURE

FIND
GOLD

The Klondike Gold Rush of 1897–98 put Alaska on the map, and still there is gold to be found, including in towns with a gold mining history. Private miners are still sluicing and panning in search of fortune, but travelers don't have to be pros to try their hands. Whether at a tourist site or on a creek, as long as you're careful not to violate someone else's claim, you may pan for gold. You may find a few flakes—some tourist operations guarantee you will! In rare cases, visitors even land a sizable nugget. Either way, you'll feel part of Alaska history.

It's easy to get started. You need a gold pan, dirt, and water. You swirl to wash away the dirt and look for shiny traces sinking to the bottom—gold being heavier than dirt. Techniques vary, but all require patience and a good dose of luck.

CHECK OUT THESE GOLD PANNING EXPERIENCES

Indian Valley Mine
This family-friendly gold panning operation occupies a National Historic Site on Turnagain Arm.
27301 Seward Hwy., Indian, AK 99540
(907) 444-6898
indianvalleymine.com

Crow Creek Historic Gold Mine
Try panning on your own or join an experienced gold miner for half- or full-day sluice-box lessons on a gold-rich creek.
601 Crow Creek Mine Rd., Girdwood, AK
(907) 229-3105
crowcreekgoldmine.com

Gold Daughters
Everyone is guaranteed to find flakes at this family-friendly operation.
1671 Steese Hwy., Fairbanks, AK 99712
. (907) 347-4749
golddaughters.com

Denali Gold Tours
Join a half-day backcountry panning tour in the Cache Creek Mining District.
9228 Petersville Rd., Trapper Creek, AK 99683
(907) 733-7660
denaligoldtours.com

AJ Mine/Gastineau Mill Tour
Put on a hard hat and go underground to tour a historic gold-producing mill in Juneau, and try your hand at panning.
500 Sheep Creek Mine Rd.. Juneau, AK 99801
(907) 463-5017
ajgastineauminetour.com

EXPLORE
KLONDIKE GOLD RUSH NATIONAL PARK

Walking around the six-block historic district in the tiny port city of Skagway, you can imagine what life was like after gold was discovered in the interior of the Yukon. Tens of thousands of stampeders arrived by ship and provisioned in Skagway before their arduous trek inland to the goldfields. Back in 1898, the city had 80 saloons, dance halls, and a rugged Old West demeanor. Fifteen Gold Rush–era buildings are now part of the Klondike National Historical Park. Stop by the park's visitor center— which occupies the former train depot for the White Pass & Yukon Route railroad (see page 37)—for exhibits and films about the Gold Rush. Parks Service rangers also lead walking tours that showcase the buildings, history, and artifacts as well as the colorful characters that spent time here.

291 Broadway, Skagway, AK 99840
(907) 983-9200
nps.gov/klgo/index.htm

SEE THE CAPITAL
OF RUSSIAN NORTH AMERICA AT BARANOF CASTLE STATE HISTORIC SITE

In the mid-1800s, before Alaska was purchased by the United States for $7.2 million in October 1867, the capital of Russian North America was a small town on the Pacific Ocean. Today the small city of Sitka is a popular cruise port. Buying the huge Alaska territory from Russia was the dream of William H. Seward, secretary of state under Presidents Abraham Lincoln and Andrew Johnson. He negotiated the deal with Russian Baron Eduard de Stoeckl. Seward's skeptical colleagues called it "Seward's Folly," "Seward's Icebox," and "Walrussia," but it turned out to be a great deal.

In Sitka, swing by the Baranof Castle State Historic Site (Castle Hill), where the transfer of ownership took place. The community still embraces its Russian culture. St. Michael's Cathedral boasts an impressive onion-shaped dome and an ornate interior with icons on display, a Russian dance troupe performs, and you can visit buildings once occupied by Russian officials.

Harbor Rd., Sitka, AK 99835
dnr.alaska.gov/parks/aspunits/southeast/baranofcastle.htm

Petroglyphs
Photo courtesy of Ivan Simonek

ADMIRE ANCIENT PETROGLYPHS
AT PETROGLYPH BEACH STATE HISTORIC SITE

On a beach in the remote fishing town of Wrangell, you will find petroglyphs made by ancient Native Alaskan peoples. Aptly named Petroglyph Beach State Historic Site, this is the highest concentration of petroglyphs in Southeast Alaska. The exact origins and purpose of the artwork is not known, though they were clearly meant to be seen from the sea. Were they some kind of communication? A sign for the gods? Directions? Merely artistic expression?

The beach has more than 40 petroglyphs in an artistic area that is more than 8,000 years old. The glyphs are best seen at low tide. Allow time to walk the boardwalk to a deck where a few replicas are on display to make rubbings. Petroglyph Beach State Historic Site is an easy one-mile walk from downtown Wrangell. Keep an eye out for Steller sea lions and harbor seals, which can be spotted from shore.

Grave Street, Wrangell, AK 99929
(800) 367-9745
dnr.alaska.gov/parks/aspunits/southeast/wrangpetroshs.htm

VISIT THE RELICS OF A SAINT
IN THE HOLY RESURRECTION ORTHODOX CATHEDRAL

Preserved under the stunning blue onion-shaped domes of the historic Holy Resurrection Orthodox Cathedral in Kodiak are the major relics of Saint Herman of Alaska. Herman was born in Russia and came to Kodiak as a monk and missionary in 1794. He was known as a defender and protector of the local Alutiiq population, establishing a school and later caring for orphans. He was canonized by the Orthodox Church in 1970.

The cathedral houses St. Herman's remains along with his monastic cap (*skufia*) and an iron cross he wore on his chest. Above the wooden reliquary is a continuously burning *lampada* (oil lamp), and Orthodox priests use the holy oil to anoint pilgrims who visit from around the world. The oil is said to offer healing to the sick and suffering. Herman's burial site at Sts. Sergius and Herman Chapel, off Kodiak on Spruce Island, is also a pilgrimage site.

385 Kashevarof St., Kodiak, AK 99615
(907) 486-3854
facebook.com/hrckodiak

EXPLORE
THE ALASKA NATIVE HERITAGE CENTER

Local heritage centers are open throughout Alaska, but travelers will find a special value in visiting the Alaska Native Heritage Center, about 10 miles from downtown Anchorage, because it is a one-stop lesson in all 11 of Alaska's major Native cultures. The center serves as a museum but is also very much alive with woodcarvers and other craftspeople, storytellers, troupes performing traditional song and dance, athletes demonstrating traditional games, and enlightening cultural interpreters.

Outdoors at the 26-acre center, a wooded walking trail along a small lake takes you to six life-size dwellings where you can learn about the traditional life of the Athabascan, Aleut, Yupik, Tlingit, and other peoples, with cultural representatives sharing firsthand stories and discussing their cultures. At the Inupiaq site, a whalebone arch is a popular photo opp. Visit the Hall of Cultures to watch traditional crafts-making demonstrations and purchase items directly from the artists.

8800 Heritage Center Dr., Anchorage, AK
(907) 330-8000
alaskanative.net

White Pass and Yukon Route
Photo courtesy of White Pass & Yukon Route

RIDE HISTORIC RAILS
ON THE WHITE PASS
& YUKON ROUTE RAILWAY

During the Gold Rush of 1897–1898, stampeders piled off ships in Skagway to make the arduous trek inland to the goldfields of the Yukon. Their two choices of paths from the Alaska port through mountain passes to gold in Canada were treacherous: the steep Chilkoot Trail or the longer, equally difficult White Pass. Soon, British financiers arrived in Skagway with the idea of laying track for a train alongside the White Pass foot trail and into the interior. Despite the obvious obstacles of geography and weather, railroad contractor Michael Heney famously declared he could "build a railroad to hell." The result was an engineering marvel, opened in 1900. Still operating today, the narrow-gauge White Pass & Yukon Route railcars take visitors comfortably up to the summit (and beyond depending on the excursion)— climbing nearly 3,000 feet. While passengers admire the tracks, trestles, and wilderness views (and sometimes wildlife too), guides share fascinating tales of the Gold Rush, those who forged the White Pass on foot, and railroad history.

201 2nd Ave., Skagway, AK 99840
(800) 343-7373
wpyr.com

LEARN ABOUT
TOTEM POLES

More than works of art, totem poles are sacred, three-dimensional history lessons, meant to be read and interpreted. Hand-carved from cedar, the creations are powerful and often tall—up to more than 100 feet. They celebrate or commemorate events and people, tell family histories, and share cultural stories and legends. They may display characters such as eagles, frogs, ravens, fish, bears, human faces, or supernatural figures. They may immortalize, or even poke fun at, historical characters. Some totem poles are painted, others plain wood. Originals and authentic replicas can be found throughout Southeast Alaska. Skilled Tlingit, Tsimshian, and Haida carvers still practice the craft. In carving workshops, such as at Sitka National Historical Park, you can see master carvers at work. Huge collections of totem poles may be visited in Ketchikan and Sitka. You'll learn more about totem poles if you see them with an Alaska Native interpreter.

HERE'S WHERE TO SEE MAJOR COLLECTIONS OF TOTEM POLES

Sitka National Historical Park

Take a ranger-led tour or walk on your own on a wooded trail to see historic Tlingit and Haida totem poles, and then watch a master carver in action.
106 Metlakatla St., Sitka, AK 99835
(907) 747-0110
nps.gov/sitka

Totem Heritage Center

This city museum is home to a rare and fascinating collection of 19th-century totem poles recovered from remote Tlingit and Haida villages. Most are unpainted.
601 Deermount St., Ketchikan, AK 99901
(907) 225-5900
ktn-ak.us/totem-heritage-center

Totem Bight State Historical Park

The park's 15 totem poles, salvaged, reconstructed, or duplicated beginning in 1938, sit amid the rainforest.
9883 North Tongass Hwy., Ketchikan, AK 99901
dnr.alaska.gov/parks/aspunits/southeast/totembigshp.htm

Saxman Native Village and Totem Park

This community has an impressive collection of two-dozen standing totem poles—including one that pokes fun at Alaska Purchase-negotiator William Seward. Young people from the village lead tours.
2660 Killer Whale Ave., Saxman, AK 99901
(907) 225-4421
capefoxtours.com

VISIT THE CAPITOL
WITH NO ROTUNDA

Built in 1931, the State Capitol building in Juneau draws visitors to its two historic murals and a replica of the Liberty Bell. What it does not have is a rotunda, the typical architectural structure covered by a dome that stands out from a distance in most of America's state capitols. (The rotunda is a style that comes from ancient Greece.)

Alaska's Capitol building was completed thanks to funds raised by residents of Juneau who wanted a home for their local government. In 1931, however, Alaska was still a territory, not a state, so there was no need for such ornamentation as a rotunda. When Alaska was declared a state in 1959, Alaskans determined that the building's style was sufficient as it stood, meeting the new state's needs without ornamentation.

120 4th St., Juneau, AK 99801
(907) 465-3755
w3.akleg.gov/index.php

RIDE
THE ALASKA RAILROAD

Alaska's iconic railroad offers views of rivers, forests, valleys, mountains (sometimes even glimpses of Denali), and the thrill of crossing high trestles. If you head to a dining car, you'll find tasty food and drink. There's also a Wilderness Café for grab-and-go meals. The year-round railroad was built by the federal government between 1914 and 1923 and crosses remote, wild landscapes on a route from Seward to the main depot in Anchorage and beyond into the Interior to Fairbanks, with stops along the way. Owned by the state but operated as a private company, the railroad carries both people and freight.

In wintertime, twice-a-week trains provide passengers a slow but enjoyable way to ride between Anchorage and Fairbanks. In summertime, daily service includes GoldStar railcars with second-level viewing platforms and panoramic viewing domes. In addition to the railroad's public scheduled service, Princess Cruises and other companies also operate private railcars for cruise passengers.

Alaska Railroad
(800) 544-0552
alaskarailroad.com

ATTEND
THE WORLD ESKIMO-INDIAN OLYMPICS

Strength, agility, balance, and endurance—all skills necessary for survival in circumpolar regions—are on display at the annual World Eskimo-Indian Olympics in Fairbanks. The games started shortly after Alaska achieved statehood in 1959, and now thousands of people head to the city's Carlson Center during the third week of July to witness a four-day competition that preserves traditional games, passed on generation to generation, as well as crafts, dance, and storytelling. Indigenous athletes from Alaska, Canada, and Greenland compete in some 50 games that leave no part of the body untested. Competitions include hopping from a push-up position using only your knuckles and toes, pulling weight via a twine attached to your ear, and a blanket toss, where the contestants are judged on height in the air and style. Greased-pole-walking is another popular event. At the Alaska Native Crafts Marketplace, you can buy goods directly from the artists.

2010 2nd Ave., Fairbanks, AK 99701
907-452-6646
weio.org

WATCH THE START
OF THE IDITAROD

The more than 1,000-mile Iditarod Trail Sled Dog Race is a grueling trek over often-difficult wilderness terrain. It's intensely cold and snowy, and the competitors need to deal with darkness, ice, and very little sleep. They compete on a sled pulled by dogs, without much protection from the elements. These slightly crazy, extreme adventure types often love their dogs like family, and that is obvious whether you watch the ceremonial start of the race through downtown Anchorage or the actual start the next day in Willow. You can also catch the teams by flying to remote checkpoints or as they cross the finish line in Nome—the race takes at least eight days, and late finishers are still crossing weeks later. The dogs are mixed-breed Alaskan huskies, which mushers will tell you are born to run. The male and female human competitors come from all walks of life. Winners gain fame—and cash prizes.

2100 S. Knik-Goose Bay Rd., Wasilla, AK 99654
(907) 376-5155
iditarod.com

VISIT
A GHOST TOWN

Deep in the Wrangell-St. Elias National Park and Preserve, at the end of the dead-end McCarthy Road, the long abandoned copper-mining town of Kennecott may be haunted and certainly is eerie. Some of its red buildings are in ruins. Kennecott was once a boomtown thanks to copper, discovered in the mountains above Root Glacier in 1900. Generations mined more than $200 million worth of ore before the operation closed in 1938. The whole town, including a 14-story mill and a recreational hall for dances, was left to the elements, though some buildings were restored by the National Park Service. The town of McCarthy, about five miles away, took care of miners' off-duty needs with its saloons and brothels. It, too, was all but abandoned until businessman Neil Darish bought most of the ghost town and got it featured on Discovery Channel's *Edge of Alaska*. Visitors drive or take air taxis to McCarthy, and then board shuttles to Kennecott.

Mile 106.8 Richardson Hwy., Copper Center, AK 99573
(907) 822-5234
nps.gov/wrst/learn/historyculture/kennecott-mines-national-
historic-landmark.htm

HIKE
THE CHILKOOT TRAIL

During the Klondike Gold Rush of 1897–1898, stampeders began their arduous trek north to the goldfields, either on the longer White Pass route from Skagway or the shorter but steeper Chilkoot Trail, a Tlingit trade route, from nearby Dyea. Today the Chilkoot Trail is open to hikers who head off on day trips to do a bit of the trail or on multiday backpacking adventures to see what the National Parks Service bills as "the world's longest outdoor museum." It's not a hike for beginners. The full trail is a spectacular but strenuous 33 miles one-way from Dyea to Bennett Lake in Canada, with nine campgrounds along the way. Plan on 3 to 5 days (you may ride a train or floatplane back). Some hearty folks run the trail. Along the way, you pass artifacts left behind by the gold seekers—everything from boots to pianos.

520 Broadway, Skagway, AK 99840
(907) 983-9200
nps.gov/klgo/planyourvisit/planning-your-hike.htm

SHOP
FOR ALASKA NATIVE ART

Skilled Alaska Native artists create an enticing array of artwork, using both traditional methods and modern interpretations. When shopping for items such as elaborately carved dance masks, silver cuffs, intricate beadwork, ivory, sandstone and baleen carvings, prints, fur mittens, and ulu knives with antler handles, you'll want to know that what you're buying is authentic. While items in shops and galleries may have a Silver Hand symbol (indicating the item is an authentic Alaska Native handicraft) or other supporting documents, buying directly from the artist adds an opportunity to learn firsthand the story and techniques associated with a piece. At the Alaska Federation of Natives Convention, held in Anchorage each October, the Alaska Native Customary Art Fair attracts more than 170 artists and craftspeople from around the state, as well as some Native Americans from the Lower 48. The three-day event is a collector's nirvana.

Dena'ina Civic and Convention Center
600 West Seventh Ave., Anchorage, AK 99501
(907) 274-3611
anchorageconventioncenters.com/denaina-center/overview

HERE ARE SOME OTHER RECOMMENDED PLACES TO FIND AUTHENTIC ALASKA ARTWORKS AND CRAFTS

Alaska Native Medical Center Craft Shop
4315 Diplomacy Dr., Anchorage, AK 99508
(907) 729-1122
anmc.org/patients-visitors/craft-shop

Anchorage Museum
625 C St., Anchorage, AK 99501
anchoragemuseum.org

Sealaska Heritage
Walter Soboleff Building
105 S Seward St., Juneau, AK 99801
(907) 463-4844
sealaskaheritage.org

Morris Thompson Cultural and Visitors Center
101 Dunkel St., Fairbanks, AK 99701
(907) 459-3700
morristhompsoncenter.org

Iñupiat Heritage Center
PO Box 69, Barrow, AK 99723
(907) 852-0422
nps.gov/inup/index.htm

(See also Fur Rendezvous, page 66 and
Raven Eagle Gifts, page 156).

HIT THE NAIL ON THE HEAD
AT THE HAMMER MUSEUM

In the small town of Haines, a museum is dedicated to a single tool. For those who like to meander through the quirky implements of life, swing by the Hammer Museum.

Worthwhile for all ages, the Hammer Museum showcases (surprise!) hammers of all shapes, sizes, and origins in the world's largest collection with 2,000 artifacts displayed in this tiny museum and approximately 8,000 more in storage. The museum is filled with history, and it documents mankind's ability to adapt to varying circumstances. Start with the rock hammers that are said to have built the Pyramid of Menkaure, and then examine ancient tools of Alaska Natives and Native Americans. The hammer, as a pounder or hammerstone, is believed to be the first major tool that man used and probably was the first tool to be fitted with a handle to increase the power of the blow.

108 Main St., Haines, AK 99827
(907) 766-2374
hammermuseum.org

SEE BLUE BABE
IN THE MUSEUM OF THE NORTH

At some 36,000 years old, Blue Babe is the world's only restored Ice Age steppe bison mummy. She's on display at the architecturally stunning Museum of the North on the campus of the University of Alaska at Fairbanks. Blue Babe is so named because a mineral tinted the animal's skin during its long, frozen burial—plus, her namers may have had legendary lumberjack Paul Bunyan's Babe the Blue Ox in mind. Blue Babe came to the museum thanks to gold miners who discovered her in 1979 while using a hydraulic hose to melt permafrost. When up popped a bison's skull, they called the university. Claw marks indicate that the bison was killed by an Ice Age American lion in fall or winter. Scientists are using state-of-the-art radiocarbon testing to learn more. The museum also houses impressive collections on Alaska wildlife, geography, and history, as well as a large collection of Alaska art, ancient to contemporary.

1962 Yukon Dr., Fairbanks, AK 99775-6960
(907) 474-7505
uaf.edu/museum

CHECK OUT A SMITHSONIAN COLLECTION
IN THE ANCHORAGE MUSEUM

Within the Anchorage Museum, Alaska's largest museum, The Smithsonian Arctic Studies Center displays more than 600 Alaska Native objects. Before they were brought home to Alaska in 2017, they were in storage in Washington. Forty elders, artists, and educators chosen by Alaska Native organizations consulted on the project, flying to Washington and going through some 30,000 items, choosing objects that represent nine cultures across the state. Most of the objects in the *Living Our Cultures, Sharing Our Heritage: The First Peoples of Alaska* exhibition date from 1850 to 1900. Community representatives also videotaped stories about the artifacts, which play continuously as part of the display. The geographically arranged items include an 1893 Tlingit war helmet, a Inupiaq feast bowl, a waterproof Yupik parka made of seal gut, and colorful masks. The exhibit also has a video installation on contemporary Alaska Native life and a 3-D sound installation featuring Alaska Native storytellers.

625 C St., Anchorage, AK 99501
(907) 929-9200
anchoragemuseum.org

SEE ALASKA NATIVE ARTIFCATS
IN THE SHELDON JACKSON MUSEUM

In a large octagonal room with a vaulted ceiling at the Sheldon Jackson Museum, an Alaska State Museum in Sitka, glass display cases are filled with Alaska Native art and artifacts. They include household items, hunting implements, ceremonial objects, baskets, and other objects collected by Jackson, a Presbyterian missionary and General Agent of Education in the Alaska Territory who opened the museum in 1897. Look above the cases to see historic modes of transportation such as umiaks (open boats made of animal hide), kayaks, and birch bark and dugout canoes. Purchased by the state in 1984 (with additional objects added), the museum is the oldest in Alaska, and the building is the first concrete structure in Alaska. Other highlights in the collection include a bearskin helmet worn by local Tlingit battle leader Katlian. There are also prized Aleut baskets with weaving so tight they can carry water.

104 College Dr., Sitka, AK 99835
(907) 747-8981
museums.alaska.gov/sheldon_jackson

TIP
Open the exhibit drawers to see collections of small items
such as ivory carvings.

EXPLORE ALASKA HISTORY
AT THE APK

Impress your friends with what you learn about Alaska's history, people, and art (past and present) at the Alaska State Museum in the Andrew P. Kashevaroff (APK) Building in Juneau. Opened in 2016 on the site of a previous museum, and named for a Russian Orthodox priest, the modern space presents facts in an easily accessible format, with archival collections, videos, and touch screens. Breeze through or slow your pace to spend hours at the detailed exhibits highlighting Alaska Native tribes and artifacts, Russian America, the Gold Rush, modes of transportation from canoes to airplanes, the fishing industry, Alaska's role in the World Wars, and politics. Pick up a map at the front desk for a suggested route through the collections. The natural history exhibits feature some 1,200 objects from seashells to mounted animals. Alaska artists get their due with galleries of traditional and modern works and temporary solo and group exhibitions.

Alaska State Museum
395 Whittier St., Juneau, AK 99801
(907) 465-2901
museums.alaska.gov/asm

WATCH
A ROCKET LAUNCH
FROM THE PACIFIC SPACEPORT
COMPLEX

Government, military, and commercial rockets and satellites are launched into orbit from the Pacific Spaceport Complex Alaska on Kodiak Island, the advantage of the location being a wide-open horizon over the North Pacific. The complex is on state-owned land on Narrow Cape, about 44 miles from the city of Kodiak. You can view the launchpads from a distance. During liftoff, you can watch what goes up in the air from a safe distance on roadways or boats. The launchpads and buildings such as mission control are open to the public during an open house held in September. The Spaceport, part of the state-owned Alaska Aerospace Corporation, has done suborbital and orbital launches since 1998. The rockets and satellites aren't built in Kodiak but arrive via airplane or barge—quite a sight when some are 80 feet tall or more.

41520 Pasagshak Rd., Kodiak, AK 99615
(907) 561-3338
akaerospace.com

CROSS INTO CANADA
AT POKER CREEK

Bragging rights come with a visit to the northernmost international border in North America, which you'll find in Eagle, Alaska. It's on the Top of the World Highway, a narrow, winding, dusty 79-mile, partially paved roadway to Dawson City in the Yukon. At an elevation of 4,125 feet, the extremely remote border post is shared by the United States and Canada— on the US side, it's known as Poker Creek, and on the Canadian side as Little Gold Creek, with both names on the building. Customs employees from both countries operate in different time zones, with a one-hour difference. The log cabin–style station is a nice photo opp. The border is open only mid-May to mid-September, 8 a.m. to 8 p.m. (Alaska time). Getting here brings amazing views of the Alaska Range, rolling tundra, and colorful wildflowers. It's a beautiful drive from the Taylor Highway connector near Jack Wade Junction.

Eagle, Alaska
(703) 921-7750
cbp.gov/contact/ports/alcan

VISIT
DUTCH HARBOR

Today, the port of Dutch Harbor, part of the city of Unalaska, is known for excellent fishing and is the operations base for the fleet of the reality TV show *Deadliest Catch*. Dutch Harbor is the nation's number one fishing port in terms of volume, primarily bringing in pollock and is famous for its King Crab fishery. Unalaska island is also home to millions of birds, some unique to the region. Traveling to Unalaska/Dutch Harbor is not for the hurried traveler as weather delays and limited travel options may make for a time-consuming experience.

Dutch Harbor history includes being bombed by the Japanese on June 3rd and 4th, 1942. The Aleutian WWII National Historic Area and Visitor Center tells the history of the war in the Aleutians, including the forced evacuation of the Unangax̂ people. War remnants throughout the island community are vastly present.

Unalaska Visitors Bureau
PO Box 545, Unalaska, AK 99685
(907) 581-2612
unalaska.org

GO THROUGH
A GIANT TUNNEL

To get to Whittier, an unusual 205-person town where much of the population lives in a 1940s apartment building, the only route is through the longest combined vehicle-railroad tunnel in North America. The Anton Anderson Memorial Tunnel is 2.5 miles cut through a mountain—an engineering marvel. It's also the first tunnel designed to withstand 150 mph winds and temperatures as low as −40° F. Initially a World War II rail passage, the tunnel was converted to add vehicle traffic in 2000. It's named for the army engineer who headed the initial construction. Because the combined highway and railway tunnel is only one lane, timing is everything when you plan a trip through. Trains have specific reserved times, as do cars. The big reason to visit Whittier is to board kayaks or other watercraft to explore the fjords, inlets, and glaciers of Prince William Sound.

(907) 566-2244
dot.state.ak.us/creg/whittiertunnel/schedule.shtml

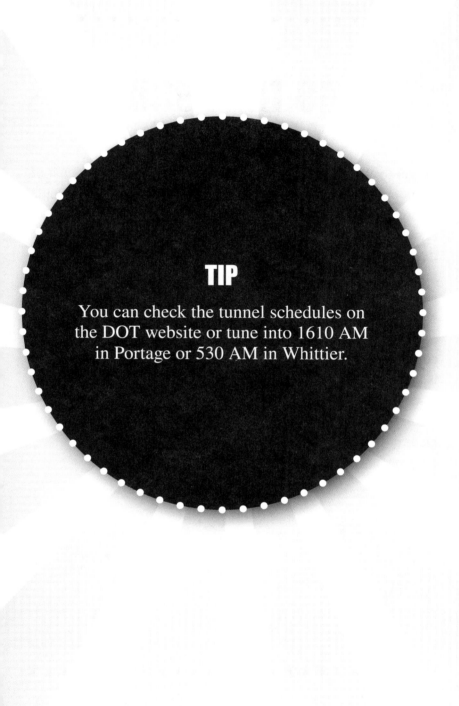

TIP

You can check the tunnel schedules on the DOT website or tune into 1610 AM in Portage or 530 AM in Whittier.

DRIVE
THE DALTON HIGHWAY

Constructed in the 1970s as a haul road for the building of the Trans-Alaska Pipeline, the narrow, mostly gravel, 414-mile Dalton Highway makes for an exhilarating, dusty and bumpy or (August to June) snowy and icy drive. The roadway runs from Livengood, about 80 miles north of Fairbanks, into the Arctic to Deadhorse and the oil fields of Prudhoe Bay. With very limited services, the drive is not for the faint of heart. Having a CB radio so you can hear reports from the truckers who dominate the highway is highly recommended. Rewards are undisturbed views of the interior wilderness—boreal forest, the Yukon River, rugged peaks, and barren Arctic plains. In addition, you experience the rollercoaster-like switchbacks of the 4,800-foot Atigun Pass, the highest mountain pass in Alaska (where avalanches are not uncommon). All this comes with bragging rights that you have been on one of the world's most remote roadways.

Alaska Department of Transportation and Public Facilities
(907) 451-5307
dot.state.ak.us/highways/dalton

TIP

Only a few car rental companies offer gravel-highway vehicles. In Fairbanks, try Alaska Auto Rental (907-457-7368; alaskaautorental.com) or Arctic Outfitters (907-474-3530; arctic-outfitters.com/dalton).

OVERNIGHT
IN COLDFOOT

Above the Arctic Circle, about halfway between Livengood and Deadhorse on the Dalton Highway, is this funky 24-hour truck stop where you can overnight in a very basic inn made out of old trailers used for construction of the Trans-Alaska Pipeline. It's a location that can see temperatures below −50° F in winter. The name comes from miners who came here in search of gold in 1900; those who gave up were the ones with cold feet. The Trucker's Café (featuring big breakfasts, half-pound burgers, and homemade chili) affords opportunity to hang out with the truckers who carry supplies to the oil fields at Prudhoe Bay. There's also a Frozen Foot Saloon. From the camp, you can take a variety of tours to explore the Arctic, including a nighttime visit to tiny Wiseman, which during Aurora season is one of the best places in Alaska to view the Northern Lights.

Mile 175, Dalton Highway
(907) 474-3500
coldfootcamp.com

TAKE A LOOK
AT RUSSIA

You can see Russia from Alaska, but only on the Bering Strait, about 130 miles north of Nome, where Little Diomede Island is separated from Big Diomede Island by about 2.4 miles. On Little Diomede, the tiny, hillside Alaska village of Diomede (*Inalik*) faces Russia. On Big Diomede, which is part of Siberia, the only people are Russian military—and since the International Date Line is between the two small islands, it's already tomorrow as you look westward. It is possible to visit Little Diomede, but it takes some work to get there. Your best bet is a flight on a mail/cargo helicopter. Tourist facilities are sparse, but the local school rents rooms—it's recommended you bring your own food. Expedition cruise ships also occasionally stop. In addition to saying you saw Russia, the other reason to visit is to purchase exquisite ivory carvings directly from local artists.

7099 School Blvd., Diomede, AK 99762
(907) 686-3021
sites.google.com/bssd.org/diomede

ToK ALASKA

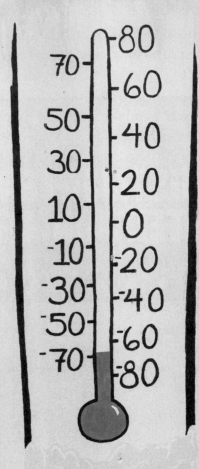

Lowest recorded (in fahrenheit) temperature at the tent in ToK was 69° below zero, in 1977

AMUSEMENTS AND ENTERTAINMENT

PLAY
AT MUKLUK LAND

Mukluk Land is a private collection of stuff turned into an amusement park, dedicated to preserving Alaska memorabilia. It's proudly tacky and fun, and it's unlike anything you'll find anywhere else. Your introduction is the "world's largest mukluk," a big red boot swinging from the entrance sign. Beyond are machinery and vehicles—engines, tanks from World War II, firetrucks, tractors, and snow machines. Peek into the doll cabin to see dolls (and eyes!) in every corner. Among the amusements are a bouncy house, Skee-ball lanes, whack-a-mole, and an 18-hole mini-golf setup. There are collections throughout, including soda cans and a ceiling covered in cereal boxes. Photo opps abound, such as a giant mosquito sculpture, a MASH tent, an outhouse with "occupant," and a red-and-white Santa Claus rocket ship. For fans of unique roadside attractions, Mukluk Land is the summertime must-do stop on the Alaska Highway.

Milepost 1317 on the Alaska Highway, Tok, AK 99780
(907) 883-2571
muklukland.com

ROOT
AT A MIDNIGHT BALLGAME

In what started as a 1906 rivalry between two Fairbanks pubs, a baseball game is played annually at the Summer Solstice (June 21), on the longest day of the year, when the sun is out in Fairbanks for almost 24 hours. Founded in 1960, the Alaska Goldpanners, an acclaimed amateur baseball team, took up the cause. The Midnight Sun Game takes place at Growden Memorial Park, starting after 10 p.m. and finishing after midnight. There's a quick twilight at about the seventh inning stretch, but by the time the last out is called, spectators will again be sitting in the sun. The welcome to official summer and cracks of the bat elicit boisterous cheers from the crowd.

PO Box 71154, Fairbanks, AK 99707
(907) 451-0095
goldpanners.pointstreaksites.com

ATTEND
FUR RENDEZVOUS

Fur Rendezvous, affectionately known as Fur Rondy, is a massive annual party in the streets of downtown Anchorage. If you want proof that locals aren't bothered by the long, cold winter, this is it. This event is about good times, with a big dose of humor. The 10-day festival originated in the mid-1930s and now includes the World Championship Sled Dog Races, with 30 mushers and their teams competing on a 25-mile course for a purse. Then there's the tongue-in-cheek "World's Largest Outhouse Race," where teams compete pushing outhouses; a costumes-optional footrace (some compete nude!); and a Pamplona-style Running of the Reindeer, where participants try to steer clear of caribou. Snowshoe softball, carnival rides, fireworks, and a blanket toss are also on the roster. Another tradition is the Charlotte Jenson Native Arts Market. Fur Rondy begins in late February and leads up to the start of the Iditarod in March.

(907) 274-1177
furrondy.net

SEE A WORLD-CLASS CAR COLLECTION
AT THE FOUNTAINHEAD ANTIQUE AUTO MUSEUM

The most frequent reaction at the Fountainhead Antique Auto Museum in Fairbanks probably is "Wow, that wasn't what I thought it would be." It's better. Owned by hoteliers and located on the grounds of one of their properties, the giant warehouse houses a world-class collection of more than 95 restored or preserved pre-World War II cars. Many are rare models, with 65 to 75 vehicles on display at any time, and all but three in the whole collection still drivable. For good measure, there is an accompanying world-class collection of vintage clothing (Parisian gowns! Flapper dresses!) that will inspire even the fussiest fashionistas. The cars start with an 1898 Hay Motor Vehicle and continue to a gorgeous 1936 Packard 1408 series dual windshield Phaeton. Visiting the place is an opportunity to step back in time in a glamorous way. Photographs and archival videos add to the allure.

212 Wedgewood Dr., Fairbanks, AK 99701
(907) 450-2100
fountainheadmuseum.com

GO ON A GHOST HUNT
AT THE ALASKAN HOTEL AND BAR

Avid ghost hunters will want to check out the historic Alaskan Hotel & Bar in Juneau, opened in 1913 and the oldest operating hotel in Alaska. Ghost sightings occur on a regular basis, even in the bar—guests may spot an image of a carriage passing in the mirror as they sip their beer. Upstairs, several rooms are said to be haunted by a young woman named Alice, who was murdered by her husband. He had headed off to seek his fortune in gold, was gone longer than originally planned, and returned to the hotel to discover that his wife was engaged in prostitution (he also murdered her client). Alice is said to appear in a bloodied white gown. Eerie orbs of light also pop up here and there, a happening that earned the hotel a feature on the Travel Channel series *Portals of Hell*.

167 S. Franklin St., Juneau, AK 99801
(800) 327-9347
thealaskanhotel.com

VISIT MORE GHOSTS

Red Onion Saloon
This bar and one-time brothel in Skagway is said
to be haunted by Diamond Lil, a former madam at
the establishment, who sometimes whispers into
the ear of male guests.
206 Broadway St., Skagway, AK 99840
(907) 983-2222
redonion1898.com

Ghost Tours of Anchorage
On this nighttime tour, look for local spirits at
local places including the Anchorage Hotel, said to
be the third-most haunted hotel in the United States.
The tours begin outside the Snow City Café, at the
corner of 4th Avenue and L Street.
(907) 27G-HOST
ghosttoursofanchorage.com

ADMIRE
WORLD-CLASS ICE SCULPTURES

Carved out of two-ton blocks of subarctic pond ice and carefully lighted for day and night viewing, the extraordinary sculptures of the World Ice Art Championships are a highlight of the winter season in Fairbanks. More than 100 artists compete, creating from ice whatever inspires them, such as fantastical sea creatures or a basketball court tribute to Kobe Bryant. Some of the best ice sculpture artists in the world arrive from the United States, Canada, Russia, Japan, Latvia, the Philippines, and elsewhere—45 countries have been represented since the championships began in 1990. Ice is forklifted into place and, from there, the carving involves chainsaws and specialized tools (some created by local master carver Steve Brice). A frozen kids' playground is part of the fun too. The event starts in mid-February, and the sculptures are on display through March (weather permitting).

Tanana Valley State Fairgrounds
1800 College Rd., Fairbanks, AK 99709
(833) 442-3278
icealaska.org

Want more proof of Fairbanks' status as an ice sculpting capital? Walk around town November through March and you'll see ice sculptures galore. And check out these icy attractions.

Ice Art Park

Kids and adults alike enjoy the mega-slides, mazes, icehouses, playground, and international ice art exhibition at this wintertime attraction, open February and March. The ice comes from an adjacent pond.
George Horner Ice Park
3570 Phillips Field Rd., Fairbanks, AK 99701
(907) 451-8250
iceartpark.com

Fairbanks Ice Museum

This refrigerated downtown summertime museum has an indoor ice slide and sculptures by featured artists, who may be on hand to talk about their creations.
500 2nd Ave., Fairbanks, AK 99701
(907) 451-8250
icemuseum.com

Aurora Ice Museum

At this year-round indoor museum at Chena Hot Springs, you'll enter an icy fantasyland created by local artists Steve and Heather Brice. Surrounded by colorfully lit ice sculptures and under ice chandeliers, belly up to the ice bar for an appletini served in ice.
Chena Hot Springs Resort
17600 Chena Hot Springs, Fairbanks, AK 99712
(907) 451-8104
chenahotsprings.com

VISIT AN
UPSIDE-DOWN FOREST
IN GLACIER GARDENS

Glacier Gardens is just outside downtown Juneau, a family run business most notable for its upside-down trees. Bright, cheerful, and colorful flowers burst from the root bases in a cascading fall of spring and summer blooms.

The upside-down gardens were the result of a moment of frustration by Steve Bowhay, owner of Glacier Gardens. Tour guides relish telling visitors the tale of how Steve lost his temper while using a large landscaping machine and slammed a fallen tree into the ground upside down. The result was that beautiful hanging gardens were planted and are now found throughout the landscape.

Included with admission is a scenic and informational ride through a portion of the Tongass National Forest. The guide shares the story of the rainforest, its ecosystem, and its importance to our environment. At the end of the tour, enjoy a snack or beverage in the atrium and Rainforest Cafe under the umbrella ceiling.

7600 Glacier Hwy., Juneau, AK 99801
(907) 790-3377
glaciergardens.com

CHEER
YOUR FAVORITE LUMBERJACK

Packed with action, the Great Alaskan Lumberjack Show in Ketchikan is a living history of the logging days in Southeast Alaska. It's also an opportunity to observe world-class athletes. Each show features roughnecks competing to be champion in 12 grueling events such as speed tree-climbing, axe throwing, chainsaw, and log rolling.

Some of the lumberjacks also compete in events such as the World Lumberjack Championships, and have wins to prove it, though they don't come easily. You'll understand when you watch their amazing displays of strength and agility. Be ready to holler and cheer for your favorite lumberjack because they love your support. The Great Alaskan Lumberjack Show is held daily throughout the summer. It's a fun family event. After the show, spectators may compete in an axe-throwing competition after some coaching on how best to make an accurate throw.

420 Spruce Mill Way, Ketchikan, AK 99901
(907) 225-9050
alaskanlumberjackshow.com

ATTEND
ALASKA'S STATE FAIR(S)

Alaska is the largest state in America, spanning more than 660,000 square miles, so it's not a surprise that it has more than one state fair. It has three, each at different times of the summer, to allow Alaskans and visitors to travel to the location they prefer. The official and largest Alaska State Fair is in Palmer, in the Matanuska-Susitna Valley. Palmer is on the Alaska Railroad system, and taking the train is a fun way to travel to the fair (and avoid the hassle of parking). The fair hosts artists, musicians, enormous produce (in Alaska, it's cabbages, not pumpkins), and all the fun things that make state fairs so memorable. Fair food in Alaska is typical, with funnel cakes and corn on the cob, but seek out local treats such as Fireweed pizza and indigenous tacos.

2075 Glenn Hwy., Palmer, AK 99645

(907) 745-4827

alaskastatefair.org

ALSO CHECK OUT THESE STATE FAIRS

Tanana Valley State Fair

The Tanana Valley State Fair in Fairbanks, founded in 1924, is the oldest in the state. It's smaller than Palmer, but has a wonderful country vibe with horse shows and animals on display. Like it's counterpart, the fair also hosts artists, musicians, an amusement park, and award-winning produce.

1800 College Rd., Fairbanks, AK 99709

(907) 452-3750

tvsfa.org

Southeast Alaska State Fair

In Haines in Southeast Alaska you can enjoy the small-town experiences from axe throwing to the Adventure Race through the rainforest. The parade ambles through downtown Haines.

296 Fair Dr., Haines, AK 99827

(907) 766-2476

seakfair.org

OGLE ONE OF THE WORLD'S TALLEST CHOCOLATE WATERFALLS
AT ALASKA WILD BERRY PRODUCTS

Alaska Wild Berry Products in Anchorage is home to the largest chocolate waterfall that you can imagine. From a height of 20 feet, the luscious milk chocolate splashes through a variety of copper pots to create a mouthwatering visual experience. The waterfall has been an icon at the store for more than 20 years. Created by Homer artist Mike Sirl, the falls are the centerpiece for the main store, which features tasty Alaska products. More than 3,000 pounds of chocolate cascade through the copper pots and splash into the waiting pool. The warming system was built specially for this luxurious treat.

Don't let the tempting smells get you into trouble by touching the melted goodness of the falls. Plenty of chocolate items are available for purchase throughout the store, which also has a good selection of other Alaska products, including jams.

5225 Juneau St., Anchorage, AK 99518
(800) 280-2927
alaskawildberryproducts.com

RIDE THE WORLD'S LARGEST ZIPRIDER
IN ICY STRAIT POINT

The bus ride to the top of Hoonah Mountain allows time to gain your courage and prepare yourself for the ultimate zip ride. Your driver will share information about Hoonah, and the Huna Tlingit indigenous peoples who are the original inhabitants of Glacier Bay. Take in the rainforest scenery and keep your eyes open for wildlife, including deer, porcupines, marmots, and bears.

Once at the top, shake off any remaining nerves, and strap in for the adrenaline rush of a lifetime as you zip down 1,330 feet at speeds of up to 60 mph. The Icy Strait Point ZipRider offers one of those moments when your vocal or silent screams are overcome by the sheer beauty of the panorama surrounding you. After you catch your breath at the bottom, be sure to stop in the Crab House for the Crabby Bloody Mary (with crab!). It's legendary.

108 Cannery Rd., Hoonah, AK 99829
(907) 789-8600
icystraitpoint.com

FROLIC ON SAND DUNES (page 108)
Photo courtesy of NPS

KAYAK IN GLACIER BAY (page 118)

HIKE NEAR MENDENHALL GLACIER (page 109)

DIVE BARS (page 5)
Photo courtesy of Juneau Food Tours

CRUISE ON A BIG OR LUXURY SHIP (page 130)

GO ON A BEER TOUR (page 22)
Photo courtesy of Big Swig Tours

GO WHALE WATCHING (page 146)
Photo courtesy of Moore Charters

GO DOGSLEDDING (page 100)
Photo courtesy of NPS, Jay Elhard, Denali National Park

WATCH THE NORTHERN LIGHTS (page 159)
Photo courtesy of Andy Witteman

FIND GOLD (page 28)

MEET A BEAR (page 139)
Photo courtesy of NPS, Jay Elhard

DRINK A GLACIAL COCKTAIL (page 18)
Photo courtesy of The Narrows

HIKE THE CHILKOOT TRAIL (page 45)
Photo courtesy of NPS

BREAKFAST AT SNOW CITY CAFE (page 7)
Photo courtesy of Snow City Cafe

REEL IN THE BIG ONE (page 124)
Photo courtesy of Moore Charters

Photo courtesy of Alyeska Resort

PARKS AND RECREATION

HIT THE SLOPES
AT ALYESKA RESORT

The great thing about skiing and snowboarding in Alaska is that winter may last 150 days or more. It's dark, though, so prepare to do more nighttime skiing or riding than you might elsewhere. The Alyeska Resort is the top place to ski in Alaska and draws both in-state skiers and those from around the world. With its fancy hotel and several restaurants (including a mountaintop gourmet spot), Alyeska has been recognized as one of the top 25 ski destinations by *Skiing* magazine. Mount Alyeska is both steep and deep. Annual average snowfall is 669 inches, and there are more than 1,600 skiable acres in the winter, with 76 named trails. Seven lifts get you to a vertical rise of 2,500 feet—including two high-speed detachable quads and a 60-passenger Aerial Tram—providing access for all levels of skiers. There are also backcountry heli-skiing options for extreme types.

1000 Arlberg Ave., Girdwood, AK 99587
(800) 880-3880
alyeskaresort.com

ALSO CHECK OUT THESE SKI AREAS

Eaglecrest Ski Area
This community owned and operated ski area has a 1620-foot vertical drop, 640 skiable acres, and backcountry access.
3000 Fish Creek Rd., Juneau, AK 99801
(907) 790-2000
skieaglecrest.com

Moose Mountain Ski Resort
The largest ski and snowboard area in the interior, Moose Mountain is 1,300 vertical feet with 750 acres of trails.
340 Moose Mountain Rd., Fairbanks, AK 99709
(907) 459-8132
shredthemoose.com

GO
DOGSLEDDING

A quintessential Alaska experience is sitting back in the "basket" of a dogsled in frigid weather, being pulled by a pack of huskies—a thrilling open-air adventure, with gear provided. In addition to being fun—your cheeks may be cold but your smile will likely be wide—the experience provides insight into Alaska history. Before snow machines (snowmobiles) were invented, dog teams delivered mail, medicine, and supplies to remote communities. Professional mushers run tours year-round including on top of glaciers (you get to the sleds by helicopter). Visiting a kennel is an opportunity for training rides (on dirt paths in summertime) and to meet the dogs and cuddle puppies who may become future Iditarod competitors. The top kennels are owned by Iditarod champions or frequent competitors who share their personal experiences in the arduous race. There are also learn-to-mush opportunities at some kennels.

GET IN A SLED WITH THESE OPERATORS

Seavey's IdidaRide Dog Sled Tours

The Seavey family, including Iditarod champion and record-holder Mitch Seavey, have been mushing for four generations. Visit their homestead for rides that range from a two-mile jaunt to a helicopter-to-glacier experience.

12820 Old Exit Glacier Rd., Seward, AK 99664
(907) 224-8607, ididaride.com

Turning Heads Kennel

This training facility is run by Iditarod competitors Travis Beals and Sarah Stokey. They offer dogsled rides at their kennel as well as glacier dogsledding tours
(you get to the glacier via helicopter).

31722 Herman Leirer Rd., Seward, AK 99664
(907) 362-4354, turningheadskennel.com

Husky Homestead

Iditarod champion Jeff King regales visitors with tales about races (he's won many). Cart rides are available in summer, as are overnight and multiday mushing tours in winter.

PO Box 48, Denali Park, AK 99755
huskyhomestead.com

Paws for Adventure

Sign up for a one-hour wintertime ride or learn to drive your own team with a three-hour Alaska Dog Mushing School adventure. Multiday overnight tours also available.

Intersection of Herning Road and George Road, Fairbanks, AK 99712
(907) 699-3960, pawsforadventure.com

Alaska Heli-Mush

Iditarod competitor Linwood Fiedler's operation greets you at their glacier sled dog camp (you get there via helicopter).

3479 Meander Way, Juneau, AK 99801
(866) 590-4530, alaskahelimush.com

PLAY ALASKA'S
GRAND SLAM

The Southeast "Grand Slam" is four golf courses in four cities. Each course is nine holes, offers spectacular views of mountains or the ocean (or both), and has its own hazards. Birds can present a bit of a challenge. For instance, the Muskeg Meadows Golf Course in Wrangell has the "Raven Rule," which states that if a ball happens to be purloined by a raven, it can be replaced with no penalty—provided there is a witness. The par-36 Valley of the Eagles Golf Links in Haines, located on wetlands along the Chilkat River, often has bald eagles flying overhead. Be prepared to also see wildlife such as foxes, porcupines, moose, and bears—and if you don't see the animals themselves, you may see their scat. Although the play season is short, the cool thing is that in summer, you can play late into the night under the midnight sun.

Whether a novice or pro, golfers love hitting the links in one or all of these scenic courses.

Muskeg Meadows
½ Mile Ishiyama Dr., Wrangell, AK 99929
(907) 874-4653
wrangellalaskagolf.com

Valley of the Eagles Golf Links
1.5 Mile Haines Hwy., Haines, AK 99827
(907) 766-2401
hainesgolf.com

Mendenhall Golf Course
2101 Industrial Blvd., Juneau, AK 99801
(907) 789-1221
facebook.com/MendenhallGolfCourse

Mt. Fairweather Golf Course
1 State Dock Rd., Gustavus, AK 99826
(907) 697-2214
gustavus.com/activities/golf.html

LEARN
TO SNOWSHOE

The great thing about snowshoeing is that anyone who can walk can do it, no experience required. You strap basket-like snowshoes onto your winter boots, grab a pair of poles, and put one foot in front of the other. Of course, if you want to go far or off-trail, there are nuances, which you can learn from experienced trekkers in lessons and guided tours.

As with cross-country skiing, going uphill and downhill requires more effort than walking across a country club or park covered in snow. In and around Anchorage, Denali, Juneau, Fairbanks, and other communities are many miles of multiuse trails appropriate for day trips, and some even for multi-night getaways with a stay in a cabin or yurt. Rentals are readily available for those who want to set out on their own.

PUT ON SNOWSHOES AND GO EXPLORING AT THESE LOCATIONS

Eagle Nature Center
32750 Eagle River Rd., Eagle River, AK 99577
(907) 694-2108
ernc.org

Denali National Park & Preserve
PO Box 9, Denali Park, AK 99755
(907) 683-9532
nps.gov/dena/planyourvisit/winter-activities.htm

Talkeetna Snowshoe Tours
PO Box 170, Talkeetna, AK 99676
(907) 733-1237
alaskanatureguides.com/snowshoe.html

Boreal Journeys Alaska
2240 Railroad Dr., Fairbanks, AK 99709
(248) 568-0345
borealjourneysak.com/snowshoeing

Leaf Out
1689 Violin Cir., Fairbanks, AK 99709
(907) 978-9848
leafoutak.com

HIKE
THE TONY KNOWLES COASTAL TRAIL

In Anchorage, the 11-mile Tony Knowles Trail (named for a former governor) is quirky, beautiful, and not at all what you would expect to find at the edge of a city's downtown. The trail takes you past the airport and into the heavily forested Kincaid Park. Along the way are views of Cook Inlet, the Chugach Mountains and Mount Susitna (known as "Sleeping Lady"), coastal marshes, and the downtown skyline.

While on the year-round coastal path, you may also spot moose, eagles, and airplanes. Chances are you'll mingle with locals—whether walking, biking, running, skating, or on cross-country skis. At about the halfway point from downtown, you'll pass Earthquake Park, site of some of the worst damage from the 9.2 magnitude 1964 Good Friday Earthquake—the largest ever recorded in North America. Other possible views: Beluga whales in the inlet and snow-capped Denali, North America's highest peak.

Municipalilty of Anchorage Parks and Recreation
(907) 343-4355
muni.org/Departments/parks/Pages/default.aspx

TIP
Bike rentals are available from private vendors.

EXPLORE
THE MISTY FJORDS

Bordering Canada and located within the Tongass National Forest, the Misty Fjords National Monument is more than 2.1 million acres of wilderness accessible only via boat or floatplane, with departures from Ketchikan, 22 miles away. President Jimmy Carter proclaimed the area a national treasure in 1978. The name is appropriate based on climatic conditions—there is a mist much of the time. On the Behm Canal, the major waterway through the area, or from the sky, views are of icy blue fjords topped by cliffs as high as 3,000 feet, tall cascading waterfalls, snowcapped peaks, and dense temperate rainforest. Deep into the wilderness are mineral springs and volcanic lava flows. While topography is the main calling card, wildlife here includes killer whales and Dall's porpoises, brown bears and black bears, mountain goats, and all five types of Pacific salmon. Kayaking the protected coves is highly recommended.

3031 Tongass Ave., Ketchikan, AK 99901
(907) 225-2148
fs.usda.gov/Internet/FSE_DOCUMENTS/stelprd3814491.pdf

FROLIC ON SAND DUNES
IN KOBUK VALLEY NATIONAL PARK

In far northwest Alaska, 35 miles above the Arctic Circle, is a sight that seems more at home in the Sahara. Within the roadless wilderness of the Kobuk Valley National Park are the Great Kobuk Sand Dunes, 25 square miles of shifting golden sand in mounds as high as 150 feet. They are a remnant of the Ice Age, some 28,000 years ago, which left behind fine sands that were grounded by retreating glaciers and blown to the Kobuk Valley. To add to the desert vision, summertime temperatures can reach 100 degrees. These are the largest moving sand dunes in the Arctic. Unique wildflowers live in the sands, bears leave tracks, and a herd of caribou passes by twice a year. To see this oddity, take an air taxi year-round (weather permitting) from the village of Kotzebue, 80 miles away, where there's a heritage center, the park's only facility with bathrooms.

171 3rd Ave., Kotzebue, AK 99752
(907) 442-3890
nps.gov/kova/learn/nature/great-kobuk-sand-dunes.htm

HIKE
NEAR MENDENHALL GLACIER

"Mighty Mendenhall" is one of the few glaciers that visitors can see without booking special transportation such as a helicopter or boat. The glacier sits on Mendenhall Lake, which was formed by the glacier over time. Stop in the visitor center to learn more about glaciers, their environmental impacts, and the flora and fauna that thrive in the rainforest. Pick up a trail map for the numerous hikes, ranging from easy to challenging. When the salmon are running, take a stroll along the platform walkways to spy a bear teaching her cub how to fish. A short hike to Nugget Falls will bring you closer to the face of the glacier to take in its majesty and to feel the brisk glacial water from the falls. More athletic hikers will want to walk the East Glacier Trail to enjoy panoramic views closer to the ice.

6000 Glacier Spur Rd., Juneau, AK 99801
(907) 789-0097

EXPLORE
ICE CAVES

It's one thing to view a glacier, but quite another to actually walk inside, admiring stunning shimmering walls of ice. The ice caves at Root and Kennecott Glaciers in Wrangell-St. Elias National Park are some of the most visited and explored ice caves in the state. The caves were formed inside the glaciers when water flowing beneath the ice created pathways. Intrepid hikers who enter a cave will be treated to views of crystal blue hues of frozen water blended with grays and muted tons of the glacier ore and silt. Touch thousand-year-old rocks and perhaps even taste pure glacial water as it pours from the icy walls.

Don't risk getting lost by heading out on your own. Several tour operators lead explorations of ice caves. Go with a professional guiding company such as St. Elias Alpine Guides.

**Wrangell-St. Elias National Park & Reserve
Visitor Center**
Mile 106.8 Richardson Hwy., Cooper Center, AK 99573
(907) 822-5234
nps.gov/wrst/planyourvisit/copper-center-visitor-center.htm

St. Elias Alpine Guides
(907) 554-4445
steliasguides.com

Spencer Glacier, Chugach National Forest
Chugach National Forest Visitor Center
Portage Lake Loop, Girdwood, AK 99587
(907) 783-2326
fs.usda.gov/recarea/chugach/recarea/?recid=71946

Matanuska Glacier Caves
Matanuska Glacier State Recreation Site
Glenn Hwy., Sutton, AK 99674
(907) 745-5151
dnr.alaska.gov/parks/aspunits/matsu/matsuglsrs.htm

SEE
A BORE TIDE

In Turnagain Arm, just south of Anchorage, there's the rare phenomenon that occurs when an incoming tide crashes into an outgoing tide and creates a long wave that travels through a narrow channel. You'll know the bore tide is coming when the water suddenly goes very still. Then comes a roar and a wall of water rising up to 10 feet high. With its shallow and gently sloping floor, Turnagain is one of the best places in the world to see a bore tide. You may also witness paddleboarders trying to ride the wave. Days with minus tides (the lowest levels) in April through October are when the viewing is best. Waves are fairly predictable. They show up after low tide in Anchorage and move through the long channel slowly enough that you can drive to get ahead—with Beluga Point and Bird Point among popular vantage points on the Seward Highway.

Viewing chart at Visit Anchorage Alaska
anchorage.net/blog/alaska-bore-tide-viewing

SOAK
IN CHENA HOT SPRINGS

When you soak in the natural outdoor rock lake at Chena Hot Springs Resort you are in water that starts some 3,000 feet deep in the earth. It bubbles up through fissures in granite rock, heated to 106° F year-round. The water is loaded with minerals (it smells like sulfur) that are supposed to cure what ails you—especially if you have skin conditions, muscle pains, or arthritis. Some say the air is good for the lungs too. Gold prospectors first discovered the springs, about 56 miles from Fairbanks, back in 1905. A rustic resort opened in 1912. For generations, people have been attracted to the springs; the experience is especially interesting in the dead of winter when it's so cold your hair may freeze while you soak—and so dark you may see the northern lights. Day passes and overnight packages are available.

17600 Chena Hot Springs, Fairbanks, AK 99712
(907) 451-8104
chenahotsprings.com

ADMIRE
THE HIGHEST PEAK IN NORTH AMERICA

Denali National Park & Preserve contains more than 6 million acres of Alaska wilderness and is home to mountain goats, moose, black bears, the fierce grizzly bear, wolves, and wild Dall sheep with curved, yellowish-brown horns. In addition to amazing views of wildlife in the wild, the top reason to visit the park is opportunity to see Denali, the highest peak in North America. A good day is when visitors capture a peek at the peak, which towers 20,310 feet and often is hidden by clouds. Visitors may drive a personal vehicle into the first 15 miles of the park, but to explore more, you are required to hop on one of the many shuttles, either a tour or transit bus. Transit buses are essentially hop on/hop off with no narration. The tour buses offer a detailed narration that explains the area, pause for views, and provide a snack or full lunch.

Mile 1.5 Denali Park Rd.
Denali National Park and Preserve, AK
(907) 683-9532
nps.gov/dena/planyourvisit/the-denali-visitor-center.htm

WATCH
A GLACIER CALVE

Watching a tidewater glacier shed, or calve, house-sized chunks of ice into the sea is an unforgettable experience. Among the easily accessible glaciers, from Juneau, you can climb on board a small boat headed to Tracy Arm to see thunderously crashing ice. Not long after departing Juneau, on the full-day outing, you'll be engulfed in greenery and wilderness. Enjoy the landscape of mountains and cascading waterfalls. Watch for bears on the shoreline. It's not unusual to view whales too.

Once the boat enters the fjord, the cliffs rise, and you may feel as if you're going through a tunnel. The captain gently and slowly makes his way around dozens of icebergs, halting in front of one of the massive twin Sawyer Glaciers. Here the boat idles so that you can watch for ice falling from the glacier's face. Look for seals in spring, when mamas are with their pups.

Adventure Bound
76 Egan Dr., #110, Juneau, AK 99801
(907) 463-2509
adventureboundalaska.com

Allen Marine Tours
13391 Glacier Hwy., Auke Bay, AK 99821
(888) 289-0081
allenmarinetours.com

DRIVE
THE SEWARD HIGHWAY

The mostly two-lane Seward Highway from Anchorage to Seward is worth the drive, even for a day trip. You're rewarded with miles of sea views and rugged mountain peaks, fjords, waterfalls and (nearby) glaciers, and glimpses of spawning salmon (from the boardwalks at Potter Marsh) in summer. In wintertime, you'll face a dreamlike white and frozen landscape. The 127-mile roadway has been designated a National Forest Scenic Byway, an All-American Road, and an Alaska Scenic Byway.

From Anchorage, you skirt the Chugach Mountains and drive into the wild. Your route takes you around Turnagain Arm, famous for its bore tide (see page 112), into the Kenai Mountains and across the Kenai Peninsula to Resurrection Bay. At turnouts, you may spot beluga whales, look up at eagles, or see Dall sheep hanging out on mountain ridges. Swans live around Summit Lakes in spring and fall. It's driving with drama, in a good way.

Alaska's Scenic Byways
dot.state.ak.us/stwdplng/scenic/byways-seward.shtml

SURF
THE NORTH PACIFIC

Yakutat is Alaska's "Surf City." It's about 200 miles northwest of Juneau and 30 miles from the Hubbard Glacier—the longest tidewater glacier in the world. Here the chilly waves of the far north Pacific, with a backdrop of spruce trees and snow-covered mountains, are the stars of the show. Yakutat, with a population of about 660, made the cover of *SURFER* magazine in the 1990s. More recently, *Outside* magazine named the place "one of the five best surf towns in America." Travelers arrive from around the world each summer—most visitors get here by air—to surf in water that may reach the mid-60s, though it can just as easily be 20 degrees cooler. The must-do stop is the Icy Waves surf shop, where you can rent boards and wetsuits, get advice from some of the 20-plus local surfers who are out regularly, and buy T-shirts to prove you were here.

635 Haida St., Yakutat, AK 99689
(907) 784-3226
icywaves.com

KAYAK
IN GLACIER BAY

You can tour Glacier Bay National Park and Preserve by small boat or on one of the cruise ships that have permission to visit. For intimate, close-up views of the park's iconic tidewater glaciers and shoreline, nothing beats sea kayaking. The bay's 3.3 million surrounding acres of wilderness ensure a measure of solitude as you paddle close enough to feel the ripples as glaciers calve sizable chunks of ice into the sea. There's also opportunity to set foot on park trails accessible only from the water. When you pause from paddling, grab your binoculars to spot bears on beaches and Dall sheep on cliffs. You may also see some of the humpback whales that visit in summer. Day trippers and backpackers may rent kayaks in the town of Gustavus for launching in Bartlett Cove (reservations recommended). Guided day and overnight tours are available.

Glacier Bay National Park Visitor Information Center
Glacier Bay Lodge
1 Park Rd., Gustavas, AK 99826
(907) 697-2627
nps.gov/glba/planyourvisit/kayaking.htm

ALSO CHECK OUT THESE OPERATORS

Glacier Bay Sea Kayaks
This small company is the park concessionaire for guided
day-kayaking and kayak rentals in Bartlett Cove (and also
offers guided multiday kayak adventures).
PO Box 26, Gustavus, AK 99826
(907) 697-2257
glacierbayseakayaks.com

Alaska Mountain Guides
AMG does guided multiday trips, from five to eight days.
PO Box 1081, Haines, AK 99827
(907) 313-4422
alaskamountainguides.com

Spirit Walker Expeditions
This company's multiday trips combine kayaking and hiking.
PO Box 240, Gustavus, AK 99826
(800) KAYAKER
seakayakalaska.com

Glacier Bay Lodge
The lodge has guided kayaking and rentals and
kayak/camping experiences.
179 Bartlett Cove, Gustavus, AK 99826
(888) 229-8687
visitglacierbay.com

RIDE
THE RAPIDS

Whether you are looking for a heart-thumping whitewater adventure or a quiet float, rafting is a great way to get into the Alaska wilderness. Gold stampeders used rafts to get to the goldfields. Modern travelers use them to get into the wild and gorgeous scenery, with views of eagles, bears, and salmon runs along the way. Six Mile Creek on the Kenai Peninsula is a popular spot for those looking for Class IV and V challenges. From Denali National Park, there are less-strenuous rides on the Nenana River. Other popular rafting locations include the Copper River in Wrangell-St. Elias National Park and the Kennicott, Nizina, and Chitina rivers. The remote "Sluice Box" on the Talkeetna River is a thrill for those looking to slam. Rafting options range from two-hour excursions to multiday camping trips, including heli-rafting.

Denali Raft Adventures

In business since 1974, this family-owned company focuses on the Nenana River, with two-hour to all-day raft trips.
PO Box 190, Denali National Park, AK 99755
(907) 683-2234
denaliraft.com

Chugach Outdoor Center

Whitewater rafting on Class IV and V rapids is the specialty, but more mellow floats are also available. The company also offers heli-rafting and multiday trips.
PO Box 28, Hope, AK 99605
(907) 277-RAFT
chugachoutdoorcenter.com

Nova Alaska Guides

Single-day trips and multiday tours range from gentle to Class V rapids.
38100 W. Glenn Hwy., Sutton, AK 99674
(907) 746-5753
novalaska.com

Copper Oar

This well-established company offers multiday beginner journeys as well as fly, raft, and hike adventures.
Old Motherlode Powerhouse
McCarthy, AK
(800) 523-4453
copperoar.com

Talkeetna River Guides

Tours range from two-hour float trips to custom and overnight excursions.
Main Street Talkeetna
PO Box 563
Talkeetna, Alaska 99676
(907) 733-2677
talkeetnariverguides.com

FLY-FISH

Remote fly-fishing in Alaska is on many an angler's wish list. You can drive or hike to rivers and streams, take a boat, or fly in to experience fishing in complete isolation. Fly-in lodges range from basic to fancy; some parks have fishermen cabins. While salmon is on everyone's mind—especially the kings (Chinook)—Alaska is wealthy with other species, including big rainbow trout. Many people head to the wide and deep Kenai River, and the connecting Russian River has its own noteworthy sockeye salmon run. The Kasilof River is known for king salmon, along with Dolly Varden and other trout. Near Juneau, Peterson Creek is a local favorite, or you can book flights to more remote waterways. The Situk River is a highly rated fishing spot near Yakutat. The Yukon River is famous for its northern pike.

Alaska Department of Fish and Game
PO Box 115526, 1255 W 8th St., Juneau, AK 99811-5526
adfg.alaska.gov

TIP
To fish you need a permit from the Alaska Department of Fish and Game.

SNORKEL ALASKA
IN A WET SUIT

True adventurers can experience Alaska like few others will dare. Snorkeling in the cold waters of Alaska is one of those bracing, good-to-be-alive experiences that comes with extreme bragging rights. Snorkel Alaska, located in Ketchikan, will schedule this immersive experience and will outfit guests with wet suits and all other equipment. The experience starts at Mountain Point to explore the tide pools and shoreline. Undersea is a rainbow world with such creatures as bright purple and orange starfish, big red sea urchins, and bright pink sea anemones. A few salmon may swim by. As you emerge from the icy waters, enjoy views of snow-capped mountains or an eagle flying overhead. Bragging rights come with saying you spent time *in* Alaska's water, not just on it.

4031 S. Tongass Hwy., Ketchikan, AK 99901
(907) 247-7782
snorkelalaska.com

REEL IN
THE BIG ONE

Fishing in Alaska is a bucket-list dream for many an angler. Catching a king salmon or trophy halibut is the stuff of fantasy and reality. The fishing season runs from May through September. Types of fish available for sport fishing will vary according to location. Plan a few days to reel in the big ones. Southeast Alaska, in particular, is well known for great ocean fishing. A charter company such as Moore Charters (owned by coauthor Midgi's husband) is equipped for day fishing of four hours to eight hours. Their favorite cheer is "Fish on!" Species to angle for include salmon (king, sockeye, chum, pink, and silver), halibut, and rockfish. Occasionally, you may hook a black cod. While fishing, you may be entertained by whales, Dall's porpoises, sea lions, and eagles.

Moore Charters
11957 Glacier Hwy., Juneau, AK 99801
(907) 723-8472
moorecharters.com

Alaska Fish On Charters
53495 Thunder Rd., Kenai, AK 99611
(907) 283-4002
alaskafishon.com

Rod's Alaskan Guide Service Fishing and Ice Fishing
3355 Repp Rd., North Pole, AK 99705
(907) 378-1851
rodsalaskanguideservice.com

Rust's Fly-in Fishing
4525 Enstrom Cir., Anchorage, AK 99502
(907) 243-1595
flyrusts.com

Baranof Fishing Excursions
3 Salmon Landing, Ketchikan, AK 99901
(907) 617-9579
exclusivealaska.com

SET SAIL
ON A SMALL SHIP

Big cruise ships with resort amenities bring more than a million visitors to Alaska each year. Small ships are popular with those seeking a more intimate, soft adventure experience. You are closer to the water, sailing to more isolated parts of the coast. Some small ships skip popular ports of call altogether, focusing entirely on the wilderness.

You'll cruise with 100 or fewer passengers and with captains who have flexibility to alter itineraries to, for instance, follow a pod of whales or give you views of bears hanging out on a beach. Most itineraries include time for passengers to borrow kayaks and paddleboards or explore on their own ashore. Naturalists, historians, and other experts provide commentary aboard ship and lead excursions that might involve getting in an inflatable Zodiac, visiting small villages, and hiking. The convivial onboard atmosphere includes open-seating meals and meetups in the lounge.

UnCruise Adventures
3826 18th Ave. W., Seattle, WA 98119
(888) 862-9991
uncruise.com

Alaska Dream Cruise
1512 Sawmill Creek Rd., Sitka, AK 99835
(855) 747-8100
alaskandreamcruises.com

The Boat Company
18819 3rd Ave. NE, #200, Poulsbo, WA 98370
(360) 697-4242
theboatcompany.org

Lindblad Expeditions
96 Morton St., 9th Floor, New York, NY 10014
(800) 397-3348
expeditions.com

American Cruise Lines
741 Boston Post Rd., Suite 200, Guilford, CT 06437
(800) 460-4518
americancruiselines.com

TAKE A RIDE
ON THE ALASKA MARINE HIGHWAY

The Alaska Marine Highway is the ferry system that transports residents, kids' sports teams, visitors, and supplies throughout coastal Alaska. During the summer, the ferry has more frequent roundtrip sailings between Juneau, Haines, and Skagway. Head upstairs to the solarium to visit with Alaska locals or fellow travelers who are also seeking an authentic Alaska experience. Bring your sleeping bag to stay warm and sleep under the stars. Some ferries have sleeping cabins; reservations are recommended.

Unlike a cruise ship, the ferry will often arrive at a town in the wee hours of the morning. Plan a few days in each town and check the ferry schedule frequently, as it may arrive in some locations only once a month. The ferry system is not luxurious, but it is necessary for those who live in smaller communities such as Pelican and Angoon, where the ferry is an important resource to transport residents and goods.

7559 N. Tongass Hwy., Ketchikan, AK 99901
(800) 642-0066
dot.alaska.gov/amhs

SEE 26 GLACIERS
IN FIVE HOURS

Seeing the blue-tinged walls of even one glacier gets you thinking about Mother Nature's magnificence. Seeing 26 named glaciers (plus others that are nameless) on a day cruise (a hot meal included) around Prince William Sound is completely over the top. Cruises on a high-speed catamaran out of the tiny town of Whittier explore up to 160 miles of the Sound, including the narrow Esther Passage and tidewater glaciers in College Fjord—where you can watch massive chunks of ice calve into the sea at Harvard Glacier and other glaciers named for Ivy League and other prominent Eastern US colleges and universities—and Blackstone Bay. Chugach National Forest Service Rangers provide the narration. Keep an eye out for wildlife that may include both resident and migratory Steller sea lions, sea otters, orcas, humpback whales, and lots of seabirds. More than 10,000 kittiwake birds hang out near Whittier each summer.

Phillips Cruises & Tours, LLC
519 West Fourth Ave., Anchorage, AK 99501
907-276-8023
26glaciers.com

CRUISE
ON A BIG OR LUXURY SHIP

With its vast wilderness coastline, snow-capped peaks, and immense glaciers, the Inside Passage through Southeast Alaska presents incomparable views from the water, including many roadless places that you can't otherwise see. Cruises, such as those of market leaders Holland America Line and Princess Cruises, are a value-packed way to see the sights with the advantage of accommodations, food, and entertainment included in your cruise fare. More intimate luxury and expedition ships from lines such as Seabourn, Silversea, Regent Seven Seas Cruises, and Windstar Cruises boost the perks (and the fare). It's easy to understand the popularity of cruising in Alaska. Without much effort, you'll view eagles and (likely) whales too, see a glacier up close, and stop at fascinating port towns. Some lines bring the Alaska experience shipboard. You may be able to sip Alaska craft beer and spirits, eat locally caught seafood, hear from local experts, and participate in Alaska-focused activities at sea.

Princess Cruises
2844 Avenue Rockefeller, Santa Clarita, CA 91355
(800) 774-6237
princess.com

Holland America Line
450 Third Ave. W., Seattle, WA 98119
(877) 932-4259
hollandamerica.com

Royal Caribbean
1050 Caribbean Way, Miami, FL 33132
(866) 562-7625
royalcaribbean.com

Celebrity Cruises
1050 Caribbean Way, Miami, FL 33132
(800) 647-2251
celebritycruises.com

Norwegian Cruise Line
7665 Corporate Center Dr., Miami, FL 33126
(866) 234-7350
ncl.com

HANG OUT
WITH (ANIMAL) MOVIE STARS

Get up close to local wildlife under the watchful eye of Steve Kroschel, who has gained a reputation as the Dr. Doolittle of Alaska. Kroschel has trained wild animals for movies and documentaries that include *Never Cry Wolf* and the PBS series *Wild America*. In 1991, Kroschel introduced Johnny Carson to a tamed wolverine on *The Tonight Show*. You can meet his animal pals in Haines at his private 60-acre park, the Kroschel Wildlife Center, where residents include a wolverine named Banff, Kitty the grizzly, and Lennox the lynx, among 15 species that also include fox, wolf, reindeer, porcupine, and a snowy owl. Most of the animals were orphaned and rescued. None are suited for release back into the wild. Many of the animals don't mind being touched. A popular photo op involves kissing a tamed moose.

Kroschel Wildlife Center
1.8 Mile Mosquito Lake Rd., Haines, AK 99827
(907) 766-2050
kroschelfilms.com

WATCH
SALMON CLIMB A LADDER

When it's time to spawn, salmon leave the sea and swim upriver, leaping, scrambling over each other, and even fighting, creating waterways so clogged with fish that you can imagine walking across on their backs. The goal of the fish is to reach their spawning grounds. They will swim up rushing waterfalls and manmade salmon ladders to get there. The mysterious trek makes for an amazing sight. One of the best places to view the phenomenon is in Ketchikan at the top of Ketchikan Creek, where an observation deck overlooks rapids and a strategically placed salmon ladder. You'll see fish, exhausted from their long journey, literally throwing themselves uphill. Sometimes it takes several attempts, and sometimes they die trying. It's a sight both freakish and enthralling, and you may find yourself lingering—despite the smell of the dead fish! The spawning season in Ketchikan is from mid-July to mid-September.

Ketchikan, AK 99901
(907) 225-6166
visit-ketchikan.com

WALK
WITH REINDEER

A private herd of reindeer will walk with you at Running Reindeer Ranch in Fairbanks. Guides explain behavior and personalities—each animal has been carefully named—as you and the reindeer meander through the boreal forest. In winter, the walk snakes through the snow even on the coldest, icy days (the animals don't mind!). The reindeer prance, leap, and stroll through the trees, rub up against your legs, and otherwise make themselves known. The herd started as one pet and became a bit of an obsession, which you'll hear about as the owners of the ranch invite visitors into their home after the walk to warm up with hot chocolate and homemade cookies. In summertime, there's also the opportunity to strike a pose in a Reindeer Yoga class.

Running Reindeer Ranch
1470 Ivans Alley, Fairbanks, AK 99709
(907) 455-4998
runningreindeer.com

OBSERVE
POLAR BEARS

Polar bears, the world's largest carnivores, hang out in Alaska in the Far North and Western Arctic areas, mostly on sea ice in the Arctic Ocean but occasionally on land. With an experienced guide, you may view these giants—males may weigh up to 1,600 pounds—during the ice-free period of August to October (September being the optimal month). The best place is near the small Iñupiat village of Kaktovik, which is within the Arctic National Wildlife Refuge on Barter Island. Here, the bears might wander into the village, especially after a bowhead whale hunt, to pick at the remains. Mostly, though, you'll spot them in the wild via guided tours on small boats (the Refuge helped develop tours that do not disturb the animals). Your best bet is to fly in from Fairbanks, Anchorage, or other towns via tour companies offering full-day, overnight, or multiday visits.

Arctic National Wildlife Refuge
101 12th Ave., Room 236, Fairbanks, AK 99701
(907) 456-0250
fws.gov/refuge/arctic

SEE
THOUSANDS OF BALD EAGLES

Up to 4,000 bald eagles fly into Haines for the late chum and Coho salmon run in November. Trees along the Haines Highway are filled with these majestic birds as they perch and wait for the buffet to begin.

Visit Haines during the second week in November to attend the Alaska Bald Eagle Festival. During the festival, you'll have the opportunity to learn all about the raptors. Experts are available from the American Bald Eagle Foundation, which is a nonprofit organization designed to educate and to sustain the bald eagle habitat. Workshops and photography sessions ensure the best snaps possible of America's iconic bird.

Other times of the year, stop by the Natural History Museum managed by the American Bald Eagle Foundation to see exhibits of more than 200 specimens of animals and plants found in Southeast Alaska. The raptor center provides "avian ambassadors" who educate the public about raptors and various other birds.

American Bald Eagle Foundation
113 Haines Hwy., Haines, AK 99827
(907) 766-3094
baldeagles.org

WATCH RAPTORS IN REHABILITATION
AT THE ALASKA RAPTOR CENTER

In Sitka, the Alaska Raptor Center is a nonprofit organization that provides medical treatment and rehabilitation for raptors and other birds. The center's mission is to educate the public and conduct bald eagle research. Birds include bald eagles, golden eagles, hawks, falcons, owls, and the occasional raven. The center is open to the public and offers daily tours. Visitors can admire the birds, hear their stories of flight, and watch them close-up.

Birds that cannot be released back into the wild due to injuries, and that can no longer feed or protect themselves, are cared for at the center. Some become part of the center's Raptor-in-Residence educational program. If successfully rehabilitated, they are released to the natural habitat. One of the most famous non-releasable birds, Lady Baltimore, can be found in her summer home at the top of Goldbelt Tram Alaska in Juneau.

1000 Raptor Way, Sitka, AK 99835
(907) 747-8662
alaskaraptor.org

Photo courtesy of Kodiak Brown Bear Center

MEET A BEAR
AT THE ANAN WILDLIFE OBSERVATORY

Ask Alaska residents and nearly everyone has a bear story, often about seeing an animal outside the windows of their own homes. Meeting a bear in the wild is another thing altogether and best avoided—especially if you're an unprepared tourist. Fortunately, you can book a tour with an armed (with pepper spray and rifle) naturalist guide who can take you to an observation area where you may watch dozens of black bears and brown bears hunt for fish. At the Anan Wildlife Observatory, about 30 miles from Wrangell and accessible by boat or floatplane, you'll hike about a half-mile to a small waterfall on Anan Creek. Pink salmon run here in July and August and are irresistible to the bear population—which you can watch from viewing platforms. Curious black bears many wander close to check you out, too.

Anan Wildllife Observatory Site
Tongass National Forest
(907) 225-3101
fs.usda.gov/recarea/tongass/recreation/natureviewing/
recarea/?recid=79154&actid=62

Pack Creek Bear Viewing Area

About a 30-minute floatplane ride from Juneau, Admiralty Island is home to some 1,500 grizzlies. Access to the National Parks Service viewing area involves getting your feet wet (wear rubber boots).
Tongass National Forest
(907) 586-8800
fs.usda.gov/detail/tongass/recreation/natureviewing/
?cid=stelprdb5401876

Fish Creek Wildlife Observation Area

This NPS viewing area is located on the Salmon River, which attracts both black and brown bears (viewable from raised boardwalks).
Hyder, AK
(907) 225-2148
fs.usda.gov/detail/r10/specialplaces/?cid=fsbdev2_038787

Kodiak Island, Kodiak Brown Bear Center

At this private center, managed by the Kodiak-area Regional Native Corporation, Koniag, Inc., guests travel by boat to view the island's famous bears.
194 Alimaq Dr., Kodiak, AK 99615
(877) 335-2327
kodiakbearcenter.com

Brooks Camp

Brooks Camp, at the mouth of the Brooks River, is one of
the top locations in the world to view brown bears.
About 2,200 grizzlies are estimated to live in the park.
Katmai National Park and Preserve
1000 Silver St., Building 603, King Salmon, AK 99613
(907) 246-3305
nps.gov/katm/index.htm

Steep Creek

This elevated boardwalk at Mendenhall Glacier is
an easily accessible place to spot black bears.
Mendenhall Glacier Visitor Center,
Tongass National Forest
6000 Glacier Spur Rd., Juneau, AK 99801
(907) 789-009
adfg.alaska.gov/index.cfm?adfg=bearviewing.
mendenhallglacier

TRAIN A STELLAR SEA LION
AT THE ALASKA SEALIFE CENTER

The Alaska SeaLife Center in Seward is a marine research center where scientists and researchers study, rescue, and rehabilitate marine animals and educate the public about the creatures that live in Resurrection Bay and beyond. At the center's world-class aquarium, you can watch sea otters frolic or observe Steller sea lions, porpoises, harbor seals, fish, and other cold-water marine wildlife. A Discovery Touch Tank is popular with young kids.

Exclusive small-group tours take the getting-to-know-you one step further. Guests age 13 and up may participate in training Steller sea lions to gain an understanding of their habits—they hang out at the center in a 162,000-gallon tank that resembles their habitat. There's also a small-group experience where you have the opportunity to mingle with a Pacific octopus, participating in feeding and otherwise learning about the brainy creatures.

301 Railway Ave., Seward, AK 99664
(888) 378-2525
alaskasealife.org

HANG OUT
WITH A MUSK OX

Alaska is full of bears, moose, mountain goats—and musk ox. Nestled in the heart of the farmland less than an hour's drive north of Anchorage is the Musk Ox Farm, home of a lively herd of more than 80 musk ox, from powerful bulls to frolicking calves. Musk ox roamed Alaska freely until the 1950s. The wild herds started to die out, and this caught the eye of John Teal, who worked for more than a decade to create Project Musk Ox, which is now the Musk Ox Farm.

A visit to the farm includes a guided walking tour with one of the Interpretive Education Guides, who shares the importance of these ice-age animals, as well as why their underfur, known as qiviut, is more than your average wool. For those who are feeling extra spry, head to the farm in mid-August for the annual Running with the Bulls.

12850 E. Archie Rd., Palmer, AK 99645
(907) 745-4151
muskoxfarm.org

LEARN ABOUT THE LIFE CYCLE OF SALMON
WITH THE MACAULAY SALMON HATCHERY

Among the 25 hatcheries throughout the state, a few are open to visitors. The DIPAC Macaulay Salmon Hatchery in Juneau is a great place to learn about the life cycle of salmon. Drop in to look around.

At the hatchery, thousands of mature salmon make their way up the fish ladder to the holding tanks, where they are "caught." Guides explain how the eggs from the female and the milt from the male are combined to begin the life cycle of new salmon. Book ahead for a VIP tour that includes a behind-the-scenes look at tiny salmon waiting to be released.

The visitor center also houses a floor-to-ceiling round saltwater aquarium with more than 150 species of fish. Kids really enjoy the squishy sea cucumbers in the touch tanks. Be on the lookout outside for a few local harbor seals who enjoy the easy pickings of salmon swimming home.

2697 Channel Dr., Juneau, AK 99801
(907) 463-4810
dipac.net

FLY TO
THE REMOTE PRIBILOF ISLANDS

Birds and sea mammals are highly attracted to the wild, rugged cliffs and windswept tundra of this four-island archipelago in the Bering Sea, about 300 miles off the western coast of Alaska and 500 miles from Siberia. Some 2.5 million nesting seabirds— tufted and horned puffins, red-faced cormorants, thick-billed murres, crested auklets, and more than 200 other species—make up the largest seabird colony in the Northern Hemisphere. Each summer, hundreds of thousands of northern fur seals arrive to breed—the world's largest gathering of marine mammals (special blinds erected on beaches allow for viewing). The islands are part of the Alaska Maritime National Wildlife Refuge. The two communities, St. Paul and St. George, with a total population of about 560, are the world's largest indigenous Aleut villages. In addition to multiday fly-in wildlife tours, May through mid-October, luxury expedition cruise ships visit occasionally.

St. Paul Island Tour
(877) 424-5637
stpaulislandtour.com

GO
WHALE WATCHING

Nearly every visitor to Alaska wants to see a whale. The waters of Southeast Alaska will host thousands of humpback whales each summer as they migrate from Hawaii with their young. Female whales bring their young to feast on plankton, krill, and herring. Summer is the best time for whale watching, and it is rare to miss the show. A good day on the water will include humpbacks and possibly killer whales. Belugas hang out in waters of Cook Inlet and the Kenai Peninsula. An especially great day at sea will include whales breaching, tail slapping, or rolling over to have some fun. Bubble net feeding is a treat, as the usually solitary humpback whale will congregate with fellow whales to feast on herring that have formed a tightly packed ball as a last-ditch defensive measure. It's not unusual to hear whale songs through the hull of a boat.

CHECK OUT
THESE WHALE WATCH OPERATORS

Alaska Galore Tours
9980 Crazy Horse Dr., Juneau, AK 99801
(877) 794-2537
alaska-galore-juneau-whale-watching.com

Jayleen's Alaska
11957 Glacier Hwy., Juneau, AK 99801
(907) 419-2007
jayleensalaska.com

Ketchikan Adventures
515 Water St., Suite A, Ketchikan, AK 99901
(907) 821-7700
ketchikanadventures.com

Seward Ocean Excursions
Seward Boat Harbor Slip M3, Seward, AK 99664
(907) 599-0499
sewardoceanexcursions.com

Sitka Sound Tours
614 Crescent Harbor, Sitka, AK 99835
(907) 752-0585
sitkasoundtours.com

Northern lights over Fairbanks
Photo courtesy of Cameron Roxberry

PHOTO OPS

GO LIVE
UNDER THE ANTLER ARCH
AT THE MORRIS THOMPSON CULTURAL
AND VISITORS CENTER

Along the Chena River, an arch made of more than 100 moose and caribou antlers is the gateway to downtown Fairbanks. But more than just the "world's farthest north" such structure, the Fairbanks Antler Arch is an iconic symbol of both nature and human life. The antlers were donated by individuals and villages throughout Interior Alaska. Collectors, some with stories of subsistence lives, found many of the antlers where they were shed—they fall off in late fall and winter, leaving space for the animals to grow new ones in the spring. One of the largest sets of moose antlers was donated by a young boy from the Upper Kuskokwim Athabascan village of Nicolai, the proud result of his first hunt. Located on the campus of the city's Morris Thompson Cultural and Visitors Center, the arch has a 24-hour webcam, so folks at home can share the view.

101 Dunkel St., Fairbanks, AK 99701
(907) 459-3700
morristhompsoncenter.org

DANCE
LIKE A CHICKEN IN CHICKEN

The historic gold mining town of Chicken is in the middle of nowhere. It has survived in large part because of its odd name and the sense of humor of its few dozen residents. Visitors arrive on the seasonal (spring to fall) Taylor Highway (#5), surfaced with packed gravel. You have arrived when you spot a giant metal chicken. Expect fowl humor aplenty—including popular "I Got Laid in Chicken Alaska" T-shirts. The town was founded in the late 1800s by gold miners who subsisted on the endemic ptarmigan grouse, which look like chickens. The word "chicken" was a lot easier to spell. The town's claims to fame include the historic Pedro Dredge and the Chickenstock Music Festival, which each June draws Alaskan artists and some 1,000 guests. The event host is the Chicken Gold Camp. Many people dress like chickens and, of course, do the Chicken Dance.

Chicken Gold Camp & Outpost
PO Box 70, Chicken, AK 99732
(907) 782-4427
chickengold.com

TIP
You can also find information at www.chickenalaska.com.

LEARN NEW USES FOR DRIFTWOOD
AT THE ARCTIC BROTHERHOOD HALL

The Arctic Brotherhood Hall in Skagway, billed as the most photographed building in Alaska, is a prime example of Victorian Rustic architecture. The unusual façade is adorned with some 8,800 pieces of driftwood found along the shoreline.

The Brotherhood was formed as a fraternal organization for gold stampeders making the arduous trek into the Klondike. The first meeting of Camp Skagway No. 1 was in 1899. The club's motto was "Ordinary Men on Extraordinary Adventures." Soon the Brotherhood had 10,000 members in 32 gold camps, mostly in the north. The organization was gone by the 1930s, but not before three US presidents, Warren Harding, Teddy Roosevelt, and William McKinley, as well as King Edward VII of England, were made honorary members. Today the building houses the Skagway Convention & Visitors Bureau Information Center. Most of the driftwood you see today is original.

245 Broadway, Skagway, AK 99840

POSE
UNDER A WHALEBONE ARCH

On a pebbled beach outside Utqiagvik (Barrow), the northernmost city in the United States, stands the Whalebone Arch, a symbol that you are at the Arctic Ocean and a reminder of the importance of whale hunting to human survival in the far north.

This "Gateway to the Arctic" is a real jawbone of a bowhead whale, which is standing on end. It's surrounded by other whale bones and the shells of traditional whaling boats.

Utqiagvik is one of the oldest inhabited town sites in the United States (there's evidence of human habitation going back to about 800 AD) and is one of the largest Eskimo settlements in Alaska. For folks who live here, whales traditionally have provided everything from meat and oil to materials for boats, houses, and artwork. Subsistence whaling is still part of life here, with captains and their crews participating in an annual whale hunt.

Near the Cape Smythe Whaling and Trading Station
Browersville, Utqiagvik, AK 99723

VISIT PROENNEKE'S CABIN
AT THE LAKE CLARK NATIONAL PARK & PRESERVE

On the south shore of Upper Twin Lake, deep in the Lake Clark National Park & Preserve, is a log cabin hand-built by wilderness icon Richard L. Proenneke. Some consider him a 20th-century Thoreau. In 1967, after an eye injury threatened to leave him blind, Proenneke at age 51 chose to leave civilization for a beautiful, roadless wilderness. A master craftsman, he built a home with a gabled roof, plus an outhouse and raised storage shed, using hand tools and mostly found materials (such as spruce logs, sod, moss, and beach stone). Over 30 years, he documented his observations about the wilderness, a lasting record of life in the wild.

The park is only accessible by floatplane (there are no runways)—with scenic flights from Anchorage, about an hour away, and Port Alsworth, about 30 minutes away from the lake. Planes with wheels or skis can land on the lake in winter.

PO Box 227, Port Alsworth, AK 99653
(907) 781-2218
nps.gov/lacl/planyourvisit/visit-proenneke-cabin.htm

SEE THE GRAVES
OF A HERO AND A VILLAIN
IN GOLD RUSH CEMETERY

The Klondike Gold Rush produced heroes and villains. In Skagway, the two collided. Jefferson "Soapy" Smith was a conman who got his name because one of his many scams involved soap. He was operating a saloon and gambling joint in Skagway when city surveyor Frank Reid had enough. Reid killed Smith in a gunfight in 1898. Hailed as a hero, Reid, too, was mortally wounded and died a few days later. It turns out Reid also had a shady past—he was wanted for murder in Oregon. Still, at the Gold Rush Cemetery, you'll find hero Reid honored with an impressive monument, while Smith has just a simple marker (and his remains are actually a few feet away in unconsecrated ground). The cemetery is a 1.5-mile walk from downtown. You can also catch a glimpse from White Pass & Yukon Route trains.

Alaska Street, Skagway, AK 99840

SOAR TO THE TOP OF THE CITY
WITH GOLDBELT TRAM ALASKA

The Goldbelt Tram Alaska is the focal point of Juneau's waterfront. Hop on the tram at sea level and soar 1,800 feet to Mount Roberts, taking in views of the Gastineau Channel, cruise ships, and waterways. Be on the lookout for eagles, ravens, bears, and other wildlife. At the top of the tram, enjoy a warm seafood chowder, crab legs, or a burger in the Timberline Restaurant. Afterward, take a walk along the groomed trails. Save time to say hello to Lady Baltimore, an injured bald eagle who cannot be released into the wild.

The Goldbelt Tram Alaska is owned and operated by Goldbelt, Inc., a native Alaska corporation. Authentic Tlingit artwork is featured at Raven Eagle Gifts, where you can watch local artisans at work. The Chilkat Theater offers regular showings of the award-winning short film, *Seeing Daylight*, a dramatic interpretation of the Tlingit heritage and culture.

490 S. Franklin St., Juneau, AK 99801
(888) 461-8726
goldbelttram.com

TAKE A SLEIGH RIDE
AT SANTA CLAUS HOUSE

Santa Claus lives in the town of North Pole, Alaska. Open year-round, Santa Claus House is all about Christmas. From the Alaska-themed tree ornaments to multiple nativities, wood carvings, and glass decor, the holiday is celebrated here year-round. Get a holiday treat at the tasty sweet shop; don't forget to order a letter from Santa.

Outside, admire "the world's largest Santa," hop in Santa's sleigh for a family photo, and plan to stop by and say hello to the real-life reindeer. Santa has them in a cozy corral as they rest up for a busy Christmas Eve. Con and Nellie Miller landed in Fairbanks in 1949 with little money and two kids. Con became a fur trader and visited surrounding villages in a red suit each Christmas. In 1952 they opened a trading post in the newly named North Pole, and Santa Claus House was established.

101 St. Nicholas Dr., North Pole, AK 99705
(907) 488-2200
santaclaushouse.com

SEE
A TINY FOREST

Adventure travelers looking for bragging rights may enjoy Adak, the westernmost city in North America. With just over 300 residents, Adak Island is part of the Aleutian Islands and is home to a huge caribou herd. Best known for Adak "National Forest," approximately 33 stunted pine trees in a clump on an otherwise treeless plain, Adak is mostly mountains and fields of low grasses. Winds are fierce, lodgings sparse, and flights to and from Adak often are canceled due to weather.

The "forest," which is not an official US national site, was begun during World War II at Christmas on the orders of Brigadier General Simon Bolivar Buckner Jr, who wanted to cheer up his 6,000 troops assigned to Adak to protect the island. Today, from a distance, the forest looks like a big bush, but according to local reports, townsfolk still decorate it annually with Christmas lights.

Adak Visitor Information
100 Mechanical St., Adak, AK 99546
(907) 592-4500
adak-ak.us

WATCH
THE NORTHERN LIGHTS

Seeing the Northern Lights (aurora borealis) in all their glory is both challenging and thoroughly rewarding. You may spot streaks in the night sky throughout Alaska, but Fairbanks is aurora central. With its location on the Aurora Circle, the city lures aurora chasers from around the world. The long viewing season here is from August 21 to April 21. Predicting the lights is not an exact science, and they tend to appear very late at night. Patience and fortitude are required. In Fairbanks, search for three nights and you have a good chance of an aurora view. You may watch for the lights from a heated lodge or yurt or while doing such activities as dogsledding or snow shoeing. Staying up late, even if outdoors in winter in subzero temperatures, is worth it when you view mesmerizing ribbons of green, other shapes and colors too, dance through the dark sky.

Explore Fairbanks
Online Aurora Tracker
explorefairbanks.com

Glacier calving in Glacier Bay
Photo courtesy of NPS

SUGGESTED
ITINERARIES

DATE NIGHT

Dine with a Top Chef at 229 Parks, 2

Drink a Glacial Cocktail at The Narrows, 18

Eat Crab at Tracy's King Crab Shack, 9

Watch the Northern Lights, 159

PUB CRAWL

Stop by Kito's Cave, 4

Go on a Beer Tour with Big Swig Tours, 22

Visit a Distillery, 14

AUTHENTICALLY ALASKA

Hike the Chilkoot Trail, 45

Ride the Alaska Railroad, 41

Try Foraging with a Chef, 20

Shop for Alaska Native Art, 46

Watch the Start of the Iditarod, 43

Visit Dutch Harbor, 55

Overnight in Coldfoot, 60

FOR THE KIDS

GET ACTIVE

IN THE SEA

Kennecott Mill Building
Photo courtesy of NPS

ACTIVITIES
BY SEASON

WINTER

Hit the Slopes at Alyeska Resort, 98

Go Dogsledding, 100

Learn to Snowshoe, 104

Attend Fur Rendezvous, 66

Watch the Start of the Iditarod, 43

Admire World-Class Ice Sculptures, 70

Overnight in Coldfoot, 60

SPRING

Dance Like a Chicken in Chicken, 151

Watch a Glacier Calve, 115

See a Bore Tide, 112

SUMMER

Reel in the Big One, 124

Fly-Fish, 122

Kayak in Glacier Bay, 118

Surf the North Pacific, 117

Watch Salmon Climb a Ladder, 133

• •

FALL

INDEX

• •

• •